SECRETS
OF A
MILLIONAIRE
REAL ESTATE
DEVELOPER

SECRETS
OF A
MILLIONAIRE
REAL ESTATE
DEVELOPER

MARK B. WEISS, CCIM

Dearborn™
Trade Publishing

A **Kaplan Professional** Company

This publication is designed to provide accurate and authoritative information in regard to the subject matter covered. It is sold with the understanding that the publisher is not engaged in rendering legal, accounting, or other professional service. If legal advice or other expert assistance is required, the services of a competent professional should be sought.

Vice President and Publisher: Cynthia A. Zigmund
Acquisitions Editor: Mary B. Good
Senior Project Editor: Trey Thoelcke
Interior Design: Lucy Jenkins
Cover Design: Design Alliance
Typesetting: the dotted i

Published by Dearborn Trade Publishing
A Kaplan Professional Company

Printed in the United States of America

05 06 07   10 9 8 7 6 5 4 3 2 1

Library of Congress Cataloging-in-Publication Data

Weiss, Mark B.
    Secrets of a millionaire real estate developer / Mark B. Weiss.
        p.   cm.
    Includes index.
    ISBN 0-7931-9358-3
    1. Real estate development—United States.   I. Title.
HD255.W393 2005
333.33′068—dc22

2004015644

Dearborn Trade books are available at special quantity discounts to use for sales promotions, employee premiums, or educational purposes. Please call our Special Sales Department to order or for more information at 800-621-9621 ext. 4444, e-mail trade@dearborn.com, or write to Dearborn Trade Publishing, 30 South Wacker Drive, Suite 2500, Chicago, IL 60606-7481.

Dedication

I dedicate this book to the world of ideas.

We all have ideas. Many of us explore our ideas. Ideas are what make humankind great. Developing real estate is based on humanity's ideas. Property development includes creativity and functionality. If most people explored, genuinely explored, and pursued their ideas, we would be a happier people.

CONTENTS

PREFACE

I started in the real estate business as a young agent specializing in commercial sales. I would, on occasion, be introduced to "real estate developers." When I met these people, I was awestruck. I was meeting the people whom I had read so much about in the real estate press. These were the entrepreneurs who built Chicago. Real estate developers were at the top of the real estate food chain.

In the early 1990s, I was invited to join the Lincoln Park Builders Club of Chicago, and, as part of the "getting to know you process," I was invited to attend their annual November Real Estate Forum. I was almost knocked over by being shoulder to shoulder with the real estate who's who in Chicago. Obviously, I held these people in high esteem. A magic surrounded them. I never thought that I could be a member of this elite group. Not just the Lincoln Park Builders Club, but the club of real estate developers.

Over the years, I have become a well-respected member of both groups, and so can you! The real estate developer's club is worth joining. If Donald Trump in this generation is the person most recognized as a national real estate developer, it's because he has a great publicist and is a third-generation real estate developer. Those are great assets, but you don't need them to join the club.

You've never heard of most real estate developers. In fact, years before Trump worked in New York, someone else had a dream about Manhattan Island. We rarely hear his name. In fact, he was discussed in an article I read while writing this book, and at the time I was not familiar with his name. I'm almost sure if you heard his name, you would make no connection with who he is or what he did. Do you know Peter Minuit? More about him later, but developers in Chicago—such as Hal Lichterman, Dan McLean, Evan Oliff, Rich Greenburg, Rich Wenxer, Harry Langer, Ron Shipka, Mark Olshanksy, Earl Malisoff, Lou Supera, Jim Crab, Patty Craig, Pat Fitzgerald, Mike Chioros, and so, so many more—are not well known. Yet they all have had ideas that changed the face of cities and impacted the lives of many.

As for Peter Minuit, he is the person who purchased Manhattan Island from the Native Americans for $24 in trinkets. His vision and ideas for what we call New York City certainly were not as grand as any high-rise luxury apartment building, of course. Yet he saw value. Many people who will never be known publicly are people who have influenced real estate development since the beginning of time. The one thing that they all have in common is that they saw value. Some real estate developers are famous and some are obscure. Some are not as prosperous as others. Many appear rich, very rich, and super rich, yet they may be overleveraged. Some are powerful people in the forefront, and some are equally powerful in the background. They are all achievers in an exciting and rewarding club. Membership is open to all people who have the dream and the drive to succeed in one of the nation's most rewarding careers. It is up to you if you want to be one of those people.

Mark B. Weiss, CCIM

ACKNOWLEDGMENTS

I want to thank my wife and son for creating the family I am so much a part of. We are a great triumvirate and have a lot of fun. Marilyn and Daniel, I don't know what I would do without you. Daniel, of course, "Tag, you're it!"

Thanks to my parents, Al and Flora Lee Weiss, for your encouragement and blessings. To Paul and Ivana Egel, I appreciate your love and support throughout the years.

I have always appreciated and respected what my associate Dan Baldwin has added with his expertise in writing skills and in life. Dan, I look forward to more adventures.

I want to thank Mary Good, my editor, for her support and enthusiasm.

Many thanks to Kathy Welton who offered me the opportunity to write books.

I want to thank the following people for their "secret" contributions within these pages: Mark Pearlstein, Linda Levin, Art Evans, Perry Peterson, Ben Weiss, and Jay Fahn.

Thanks to the Lincoln Park Builders of Chicago who allowed me to serve as their president from 2000 to 2002.

And thanks to the following people who have had a valuable impact and assisted me through the years: Richard Reizen, Dan Loewenstein, P. Jerome Jakubco, Terry Engel, Robert Griffiths, Carter Huhta, Peter J. Haleas, Ryan Cooley, Brian Griffin, and Dan Starzyk.

Industry Overview

There are two things to aim at in life: first, to get what you want; and after that, to enjoy it. Only the wisest of mankind achieve the second.

Logan Pearsall Smith

Although I've never counted myself among the wisest of men, I know I am doing a good job of getting what I want out of life. A big part of that joy is enjoying my ability to do well in my chosen profession, real estate development. You should know that I am not exclusively an author of real estate books, although this is my fifth published work. The opportunity to write real estate books presented itself as a new opportunity based on my reputation as a successful real estate developer, broker, and property manager in Chicago. I believe in the theory that "when opportunity knocks, open the door." I felt this medium would allow me to share my creative ability to communicate the real estate lessons I've learned over the years. My real estate career and my attitude have allowed me to build a good quality of life. I have a happy, healthy family and a job that I love immensely. Much of that joy, job satisfaction, feeling of achievement, and the thrill of taking on new challenges is due to the simple fact that my career choice was real estate and real estate development.

The insights I share in this book can help you achieve success and enjoy your life. Success in real estate is accessible to virtually everyone in the free world. The real estate industry is amazingly open. For centuries, individuals and families have chosen to enhance their income or even build fantastic wealth through real estate.

Look at it this way. We all live in, work in, shop in, and walk the dog on real estate. We shop in malls and shopping centers, go to work in office buildings, warehouse our goods in industrial buildings, create products in manufacturing facilities, and build dreams on raw land. During our lifetime, we will live in two or more dwellings. These may be apartments, single-family dwellings, condominiums, or co-ops. We may spend our golden years in our own home, in the home of our children, in a nursing home, or in an assisted living facility. Regardless of how we classify them, these types of properties all involve real estate development. Real estate development is everywhere, and that means people are buying and selling real estate everywhere.

Unless you're a government agency, a religious facility, or a charitable agency, the type of transaction I'm referring to is for-profit real estate development. The individuals, families, companies, and organizations buying and selling all this real estate do it for one primary reason and that is to earn a good return on an investment. As a rule, you'll find developers are people with ambition, incredible energy, and vision. There's lots of room for more people like that, too. Are you one of them?

Think about it. Even in the worst recessions, real estate development has never stopped developing. Things may have slowed down now and then, and, as with any industry, there are ups and downs in the economy, but throughout the history of this country, real estate development has never come to a standstill. Other industries can't make that claim. Consider the stock market. During the 1990s, the stock market was, financially speaking, *it.* I know people who were earning 10, 15, 20, and even 50 percent on their stock market investments during the bull market in the late 1990s. I'm not against diversifying your investments with a few stocks or mutual funds, mind you, but I do know something about financial history. Every time a balloon goes up, at some point it bursts. Consider a few things from past headlines. I think you'll remember some of these stories.

During year 2003, bankruptcies reached record levels. The energy company Enron announced one day that it was worth $1.2 billion less than it had stated. WorldCom filed bankruptcy in 2002 because of over $11 billion in financial irregularities. Martha Stewart was indicted for insider trading on Wall Street in 2004. Global Crossing, a huge telecom company, filed for what became the fourth largest bankruptcy in American history. The country's sixth largest cable company, Adelphia, filed for bankruptcy. Merrill Lynch paid a $100-million fine after being accused of promoting worthless stocks. Some of the nation's top mutual funds have been accused of trading abuses in New York, including Janus, Bank of America, Putnam, Bank One, and others. And these are just the big cases that grab page one headlines. There were many others.

The recession of 2000–2003 that was in part caused by these scandals hammered America's investors. Tens of millions of people saw their investments, retirement funds, life savings, college funds, and so on go right down the toilet with the economy.

During that same time, tens of millions of Americans did not lose their savings in real estate. Certainly the recession had an impact, but the real estate engine never stopped chugging along. Can you say that about the companies involved in the stock market scandals? The real estate engine roars on because it has real fuel—the vision of real estate developers. And that's why it will never cease to be a powerful means of building real wealth and security.

Real Estate Development and Real Estate Needs Are Not Necessarily the Same Thing

The U.S. population is currently expanding at a rate of about 1,000,000 people a year, about 10,000,000 additional people every ten years (births minus deaths plus immigration). The numbers may vary as time goes on. People are living longer. From time to time immigration figures expand or contract, but I don't see that number of annual expansion dropping below the 1,000,000 mark. If anything, the expansion may increase as time goes on. That means a lot of people will be looking for places to live—real estate. More than that, they'll be fueling our economy with demand for all kinds of goods and services. Thus business needs facilities to produce, deliver, and showcase those products and services—more real estate. Business-to-business enterprises will form or expand to meet those needs—even more real estate. That's going to happen regardless of any ups and downs in the economy because, one reason among many, downward economic cycles and recessions do not end demand for goods and services. When demand for housing is present, demand for durable goods, such as appliances carpeting, household lighting fixtures, picture frames, paint, porcelain, pots and pans, in fact everything for the home, is present also.

People and jobs drive real estate development *needs,* not necessarily real estate *development.* Despite the verbal similarity, they're two completely separate things. *Real estate development need* is what energizes the vision of the developers. It's what they think about, dream about, read about, and it's what the demographic reports describe. This real estate development *need* fuels many other needs and objectives of the population. *Real estate development* operates on a different level, the level of the profit center. It's a way of doing business. The two are intimately related, but they run on entirely separate tracks.

Real estate development often exceeds real estate need. How does this happen? The answer is basic economics, and excess development teaches a good lesson in how even savvy developers can ignore basic and obvious business rules. You see it all the time in your local newspapers. For example, let's say a respected demographer reports to a local business group that the area will soon be in need of 1,000 new homes to accommodate expected growth. Area developers jump on that news and start building. Five developers or more start pouring concrete, hammering nails, sawing boards, and nailing down roofing tiles. Soon the city doesn't have 1,000 new homes; it has 5,000 or more new homes. If the developer community is aggressive, it could put up 10,000 or more homes before someone realizes that the town is grossly overbuilt. Supply exceeds demand, and this dynamic is especially hard on the developers who started building toward the end of the frenzy.

We saw this in the late 1990s in River North, an area on the north side of Chicago that during the past 30 years has become a highly desirable area for business, recreation, and entertainment. We all realize that time is a precious commodity. It's really all we have, and the less time we spend getting to and from work, the more we have for the more pleasurable, profitable, and productive areas of life. River North is close to Chicago's Loop, making it an ideal area for housing development.

Developers know a good thing when they see it, and many of them jumped feet first on this bandwagon. Construction boomed, and condominiums began going up throughout the entire neighborhood. Like flowers at springtime, thousands of condos were bursting up out of the ground. High-rise condos can take up to three years to build, and development time is where the problems started showing up. By the time many of these buildings were topped off, supply had already exceeded demand. Many of these buildings went immediately into foreclosure, causing major financial problems for the developers. Those without deep pockets had serious financial problems.

Of course, the fact that there was overbuilding in River North doesn't mean that there was overbuilding in other parts of the city. In fact, neighborhood infill projects, projects that were filling gaps in existing neighborhoods, were doing quite well. The suburban developments of town homes, condominiums, and single-family homes were doing well, too. The absorption rate, the rate in which units are sold during their marketing period, was good. River North was Chicago's hottest hot neighborhood. Where the market is perceived to be hot, many will build. In areas that were stable and less sexy, condominium units continued to sell steadily to a conventional market.

☛ **SECRET OF A MILLIONAIRE REAL ESTATE DEVELOPER**

1. Know how to read your market.

It's important to know when to hold off for a while and stop building. You can learn that lesson from reading this book. I learned through experience, maturity, hard knocks, and the disappointment of occasionally not making as large a profit as I had projected.

My friends and associates have all experienced the same thing. My disappointments have not been substantial. But you must know that the important thing in being successful is to learn to move on. Losing money—by paying too much for services, not figuring your sales prices accurately, or through any error that costs you money—is your tuition to success in real estate development. Unless you are born into the lucky-breaks club, you will make it or break it on your own.

It is important for you to know that it is normal for people to tell you they have never lost money in a real estate deal, even though they have. People don't like to admit their vulnerabilities. Their ego is at stake. The bigger the deal, the more potential exists for bigger losses.

I can also tell you from personal experience that I have never had a project come in on time. Despite my best efforts and the best efforts of very professional teams, I also have never maintained my projected budget. My sales figures have never been where I expected them to be. Still, every one of my projects has been profitable. My point? In real estate, there's lots of room for error. That doesn't mean you should play the margins, get sloppy in any area, or just trust blindly to luck. You can get hammered in real estate just as hard as you can in the stock market. It's just that my crystal ball has always been a bit cloudy and that will be your case, too. And that's all right. If you have the vision, you can still see your way to a successful real estate career.

A Word of Warning about the Secret of Success

Here's an important secret. A word of warning actually. Sometimes a newcomer's first project beats the odds and goes to a successful completion on time, on budget, with no hassles, and makes good money. That's great, but there's a real danger that the new developer will think things fall into place like that all the time. *They don't.* Most of the time your projects won't meet your expectations. Real estate development is simply a reflection of most things in life. We strive for perfection and settle for less. That is normal. Life is like that and so is real estate. Deal with it.

 **SECRET OF A MILLIONAIRE REAL ESTATE DEVELOPER**

2. Know how to deal with difficult and unexpected situations.

Commercial Real Estate

Any type of real estate that is not residential and is not industrial can be considered *commercial* real estate. It's an extremely broad category that includes single businesses, strip shopping centers, large shopping centers, fast food restaurants, office complexes, and retail malls comprising hundreds of thousands of square feet. The key warning I made concerning supply exceeding demand in residential construction applies just as well in commercial real estate. Ten developers hear that an area needs 1,000,000 square feet of commercial space. They all start building, and in no time at all the community has 10,000,000 brand new square feet of retail space, and 9,000,000 of those square feet are vacant.

Smart commercial developers hedge their bets by using a technique called preleasing. *Preleasing* is having a tenant committed to occupy a space prior to construction. Having the space preleased guarantees you and your lender that the project will be successful. For now, just realize that there are many options available to the savvy developer and that you'll learn them in this book. Overbuilding is a very real problem in commercial real estate. We see it all the time, often in five-year cycles. Back in the early 1990s, it seemed like every corner in Chicago had a new bagel shop. A decade later, there seems to be a new bank on every corner. A developer sees someone else's success at a location and thinks, "Hey, I can do that." In short order a competitor moves in. Then another developer sees what's going on and decides to jump on the bandwagon. Obviously, every four-corner intersection can't support four banks, four bagel shops, four coffee shops, or four of just about any commercial enterprise. Yet, this trend will continue, and you'll have to maneuver your way around it on your way to becoming a millionaire real estate developer.

Industrial Real Estate

Industrial markets in this country are constantly changing. That's because the needs of the nation are evolving. At one time, we manufactured things in large, complex, loud, and often dirty plants where we produced steel pipe, gas turbines, planes, trains, and automobiles. Think of the movies from the early twentieth century that featured those belching smokestacks, production lines stretching into infinity, and long lines of workers in coveralls marching towards the time clock. Today, a manufacturing plant is more likely to be clean, efficient, well-organized, and often rather quiet. Take a tour of a facility that makes computer chips, telephones, or any type of electronic equipment to get an idea of what I mean. To adapt a line from an automobile commercial, "This ain't your dad's manufacturing floor."

Things have changed and not only have they changed quickly, they have changed radically. In those "good old days" we employed people to knit, sew, hammer, saw, bolt, and assemble. This was primarily piecework. Industrial buildings were usually multilevel structures located within the city. People lived nearby, and the trip to and from work was quick, simple, and easy. Entire communities lived around the plant. Often several generations of families worked "down at the mill." People went to the same churches, schools, city parks, and stores, and they developed a real sense of community.

Well, we're in the "good new days" now. Americans don't really manufacture many large and heavy products anymore. We're into light manufacturing and high-tech products. Many of our goods are made overseas and warehoused here. Progress has dictated all kinds of changes that directly affect real estate, many of them you'd probably never consider. For example, because inventory is stored rather than manufactured here, buildings need higher ceilings to accommodate inventory stacked on pallets. New construction by real estate developers has to take such matters into consideration.

In many cases, existing construction has become out-of-date for modern industrial needs. You can't raise the ceilings of a large, multistory building downtown. Fortunately, the real estate industry is filled with men and women of true vision. We don't look at an abandoned building and see the emptiness. We see the opportunity. Take all those abandoned manufacturing plants in the nation's downtowns. People of vision created an entire new type of real estate entrepreneur—the residential loft developer. This type of development is called "adaptive reuse." These buildings, no longer of any use for manufacturing, could be adapted to reuse as living spaces for the emerging residential needs of the community. The urban condominium loft so common across the nation is a direct result of this kind of visionary thinking.

Opportunities for Today and Tomorrow

A millionaire real estate developer knows, understands, and appreciates the fact that opportunities are always changing. Legend has it that those adaptive reuse condominium loft buildings I just mentioned started in New York after World War II. As industry left the city, the buildings were recycled to provide inexpensive housing. The properties were especially popular with artists and people running small businesses catering to urban markets. People who couldn't afford to own or rent a house while at the same time own or rent a place of business suddenly had a new and exciting option. They could work and live in the same property. Thus the work/live space of the twentieth century came into its own.

Certainly, the owners of these large buildings were delighted to earn any kind of income from them. Later on, many of these same properties, which had been rented out at very low rates, were converted to condominiums that would bring in hundreds of thousands or even millions of dollars of real estate income. We don't know who created the first condominium loft development, but we see the product of that genius everywhere. The concept isn't limited to recycled buildings. Many new properties in urban centers mirror the vintage nature of their predecessors.

One of my favorite aspects of real estate development is the creative niche. I'm certainly not one of the nation's megadevelopers, but I have found my very own spot. I've created a niche where I can conduct business, help people, take care of my family, grow, and prosper. I also like the fact that there are numerous niches waiting to be filled or to be created by someone with the vision to do so. I love finding a property that no longer meets the needs of the twenty-first century, conceiving of a way to put it to good and profitable use, and then turning that vision into a reality. There's no feeling in the world like that. While writing this book, I developed two such properties.

One of our greatest visionaries looked on some acreage around Anaheim, California, and thought it a good place for his new concept. He did not realize at the time that he was creating what is now called a "theme park." As you know, his name was Walt Disney. I doubt that even he had a vision of just how dramatic an impact his idea would have on the nation. Today, families from all over the world enjoy Disneyland, Walt Disney World, Universal Studios, Six Flags, Lego Land, and thousands of other parks and entertainment venues. The impact of a single development is often communitywide. Cities create new infrastructures to lure or support these businesses. Hotels, restaurants, shopping centers, gas stations, convenience stores, and other businesses sprout up to serve the needs of the tourists. Other businesses then sprout up to serve the needs of the people serving the needs of the tourists. Talk about your basic win/win scenario!

All of this positive impact sprang from the mind of one man with an idea and the commitment to make it happen. That's what real estate development is really all about. When I first visited Walt Disney World in 1972, Orlando, Florida, was still a small town. The only area open to the public at that time was The Magic Kingdom. If you've been to Orlando in recent times, you know that it's become quite a city. There are thousands of hotel rooms on the Disney property alone, and the company itself employs 55,000 people.

I can't even begin to imagine how many people work just at the international airport, shopping centers, hotels, service businesses, and the residential communities. Think of the school teachers, bus drivers, store clerks, doctors, lawyers, and aspiring actors who wouldn't have those jobs today if Walt Disney hadn't come along. That's what I mean by real estate vision. A single idea, often a surprisingly simple one, will spring forth from a creative mind to spur great expansion, create jobs, build communities, and change lives. The theme park concept makes a lot of sense with the advantage of hindsight, but back then only the most creative minds looked at raw land and saw the amazing opportunities for tomorrow. That's the real fun of real estate development. You not only participate in the future, you have a hand in creating it.

Potential Obstacles Today and Tomorrow

You'll encounter many obstacles in your real estate career. I've already mentioned missing deadlines, blowing budgets, and the dangers of over-building. Regardless of the challenge, there's usually a way to go over, under, around, or right through it.

Always take time to thoroughly research any project you're considering. I encourage people to invest a year in research before committing to a first real estate project. Believe me, that's not too long a time frame. No project is worth rushing. And if you miss an opportunity, another and another and another will always come along.

I'm a big believer in seeking advice and counsel from people who are in the know, and you'll read that advice throughout much of this book. Here's an important add-on to that recommendation.

 SECRET OF A MILLIONAIRE REAL ESTATE DEVELOPER

3. Ultimately, you must follow your own gut instinct.

I seek out and listen to the advice and counsel of businesspeople I trust. But opinions vary and are often contradictory. If you doubt me, tune in to one of the many stock market and financial shows on television to see just how widely experts can disagree and how far off the mark their opinions can land. In the end, it's always your decision. Always follow your own gut instinct. I will repeat that theme throughout this book as I do in my other books. Following your intuition most times will lead you to success. Because your inner voice speaks, remember to listen to your own good judgment.

We all make good judgments and bad judgments, and this book is full of both instances from my own experience. For example, when I was building my first new construction project, I bought a piece of land I knew would allow me to build 12 dwelling units above a retail space. As with most developers, I wanted to enhance my profit picture. Eighteen units would do that nicely, I reasoned. To build those additional units, I had to apply through the appropriate channels for a zoning change. It appeared that many developers in Chicago have done this successfully, so why couldn't I? Because I had never gone through this process before, I asked one of Chicago's top zoning attorneys, who happened to have been a neighbor while I was growing up, to shepherd me through the process. How could I go wrong with a longtime friend who was a well-respected professional?

At the time, the alderman (city councilman) for the ward in which my property was located was up for reelection. This was a hotly contested race. I called the alderman, and she suggested that the proper first step through the zoning change process would be to talk to the neighborhood block club or community group. If they supported the change, she would back my plan. My timing could not have been more wrong. Worse, I followed the direction of my very powerful and well-known and expensive zoning attorney every step of the way.

My fatal mistake was to move too quickly. The alderman was playing it safe and wasn't about to do anything that might have a negative impact on her reelection. She wasn't about to get involved in my project. Not because it was controversial, only because in politics the smart thing to do in an election is to avoid getting involved in anything new until you have won and are in your "safe seat." I remember being taught this concept in political science class in college. Had I paid more attention in class, I would have waited until she won and was sitting in that safe seat, or until a new alderman was in position. Yet, my all-knowing attorney encouraged me to move right in and meet with the neighborhood group.

That, too, considering the timing of the meeting, was a horrible mistake. The group had just elected a new leader, but one who was unpopular within the community. The first task on his to-do list was to address my development project. Well, despite all my high-powered advice from my attorney, everything went from bad to worse. I invested thousands of dollars in attorney fees, architectural fees, and hours of humiliating frustration in front of this group for nothing.

☛ SECRET OF A MILLIONAIRE REAL ESTATE DEVELOPER

4. Only those who oppose your development will show up at community meetings.

The opponents are always vocal. Your supporters take it for granted that you will get what you want. You will never see a screaming mob of people who say, "Yes, build that in my neighborhood." Those who attend are members in NIMBY (Not In My Back Yard). That's who showed up at the community meetings, those loud vocal people who wanted no change. They won.

Then, things changed. Right after the alderman won her reelection, she called me. She wanted a meeting to discuss zoning changes that would allow for more residential units in properties such as mine. She had a hidden agenda. She'd allow me more units if I'd designate 10 percent of the units to a new city initiative she was heading up. That initiative, in the formative stages at the time, would have provided affordable or lower priced housing in 10 percent of the units. If I built 30 units, which was what would have worked and been most generous, the alderman would have had a showplace for other developers.

Had I just waited until after the election, I probably could have walked into those group meetings and through the zoning process with the support of the alderman and walked out with pretty much whatever I wanted or close to it. Unfortunately, I had listened to my brilliant, high-priced, experienced, and high-powered attorney who at the end of the day got paid and walked away. This was a valuable but costly lesson. I laugh at it now because I realize that in many cases the emperor has no clothes. The big shot ain't always so smart. Or so big. Learn from my mistakes. Politics operates on the basis of its own logic, and that logic is often built around reelection.

Realize as an unalterable fact of life that the professionals you consult are not thinking about your pocketbook. Architects often design to satisfy the needs of their own egos rather than the needs of your market, community, or budget. Lenders are very happy to lend in order to get points and fees and interest from the loan, but they will not always carefully review your financial figures and tell you whether or not you're under or over budget. The construction manager or general contractor may eat into your profits by charging you invisible fees under the line item of "general conditions." Contractors may not provide the proper lien waivers or even pay their subcontractors. And those subcontractors may not show up on the job site, may not do the work as directed, may make improper charges, or they may even go out of business during your project's construction. Obviously, the attorney you consult on zoning matters may not know what he's talking about.

During the 1980s, President Ronald Reagan was dealing with the fall of the Soviet Union. In his dealings with communist leaders, he developed a policy that was beautifully phrased. Reagan's words, found in the following secret, apply to real estate development as well as international diplomacy.

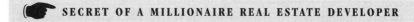

SECRET OF A MILLIONAIRE REAL ESTATE DEVELOPER

5. "Trust, but verify."

That's an essential policy when dealing with other people in business. Regardless of whom you trust, verify everything. Let me repeat that, verify everything! You will be dealing with thousands and hundreds of thousands of dollars. Some of you will be dealing with millions of dollars. I've seen developers completely trust (without verifying) the people on their staff, their support teams, such as attorneys or construction companies, and the advice of trusted professionals only to get caught in a financial catastrophe.

People are seductive. They want you to like them, to trust them, to believe them, and to run with the advice they provide. This can be dangerous ground for the novice developer who has not yet learned the listening skills needed to survive.

When applying for a building permit some years ago, I trusted, but did not verify, the word of an architect, who came to me by way of a strong referral. He seemed trustworthy, and he certainly knew my target area in Chicago. Getting the project rolling depended on him assisting us in getting a building permit. I needed all the help I could get because the City of Chicago Department of Buildings was in chaos. There was a time when we went through four different building commissioners in six years. Such a lack of continuity is bad business for the city, the city's developers, the people who depend on the developers for their living, and ultimately for the citizens who need the developers' properties.

The process of obtaining a building permit was long, complex, and arduous. Again, this is why I needed the expertise of the architect. Because I did not verify his actual progress at the Department of Buildings, I didn't realize he was very busy building his own business and he let my little project just fall through the cracks. For example, when the city sent plans back to him for corrections, he should have completed the task and returned the documents in no more than a few weeks. Instead, the permit plans actually took up lodging on his desk for months.

I didn't think anything was out of place because at the time it was not unusual to hear from developers, architects, lenders, and anyone else in the business that the permit process was taking a year or more for everyone applying for a building permit at the time even for the smallest renovation or repair. Because I was comfortable with what I believed were common delays, I missed the fact that my architect was just lying to me. He kept saying that the permits were "just weeks" from being granted.

I finally checked things out on my own down at city hall where I discovered that he had just sat on my permits from August to March of the following year. I sued him for malpractice and fortunately for his business he had substantial insurance. We are still litigating the case while I'm completing this book. I wrote five books during the period of discovery of this "professional's" behavior, and we have not yet settled the case. I know that we will settle the matter in my favor with a monetary award because he is insured and we have significant evidence from the City of Chicago Department of Buildings showing his negligence. This architect's attitude is all too common, and it never fails to amaze me. Because of his laziness or indifference or whatever, he lost a lot of money, had his insurance rates go up, was embarrassed in the professional business community, and I lost three-fourths of a year off my project. And all he had to do was—do his job.

Don't believe that just because you have a contract with a supplier that you are fully protected. The courts are full of contract disputes, and good does not always triumph over evil. Even suppliers who sign contracts in good faith and who have every intention of fulfilling their obligations can experience circumstances that may make them fail in those obligations.

☞ **SECRET OF A MILLIONAIRE REAL ESTATE DEVELOPER**

6. Get lots of referrals on your suppliers and then carefully check out those referrals.

Once you find good and reliable contractors, stick with them. Even if they cost you a bit more than their competitors, stick with them. The best suppliers can never compete just on price because someone else can always make a lower bid. The low bidder isn't always the best supplier, and the low bidder also may be incapable of finishing the job to your specifications.

Considerations for the Newcomer

For many very sound reasons, my advice to beginning real estate developers is to start small. There's a reason you see so many small developers and so few large ones. Big, expensive, and complex projects are an entirely different risk game. When or if you ever decide to move up to bigger leagues, then do so carefully and cautiously. You can begin by using your own money. You'll gain a lot of knowledge and experience, and you'll make a lot of mistakes. But you'll grow quickly. Also, working on your own eliminates the burden of reporting back to partners. You can make decisions quickly and respond to changing market conditions faster than partnerships or syndications can. Many developers like the "lean and mean" side of the business so well that they remain small developers throughout their careers. Please note that small businesses or projects don't necessarily mean the size of your profit is correspondingly small.

A newcomer needs to quickly grasp an understanding of the following five areas:

1. Locate the real estate you want to develop. You need to tie up the property with a strong contract that allows you to buy it and close on the sale. This contract needs to include all the contingencies you need so you can fulfill the needs of your development.
2. Have or acquire the money necessary to make the deal work. You need the initial equity to get the transaction going, and then you need the loan to conclude that transaction.
3. A developer must have the construction capabilities to develop. You need the men and women, material, and machines to carry the project through to completion.
4. An exit strategy is essential. This means knowing precisely what you're going to do with the property once you've completed your construction. Are you going to sell it or rent it?
5. Consider what you intend to do with the money you make from the sale or the rental. How will your profits affect your business, your plans, and your tax liabilities?

These five items are just general guidelines, but no real estate development plan should be without them. Of course, you'll have to flesh them out with details, specifications, budgets, timetables, estimates, and so on. It's critical to understand that regardless of how carefully you calculate your estimates (time, money, personnel, supplies), the final numbers will be different. That's because you can never fully plan for the unknown. You may experience construction delays, weather problems, permit delays, partners who pull out at the last minute, price increases for raw materials, a need for additional funds, lenders who change the terms of the agreement, and any number of other major and minor catastrophes. It's wise to include contingencies to cover the unexpected because bad news in some form will always come knocking on your door.

Take your time in looking for a property to develop. In every real estate book I have written, I urge people to invest at least a year in the search for the first property or project. After the first project, you will know what you are doing; still needing to learn of course, but you will have experience. That's sound advice for the experienced professional, and it is essential advice for the novice. You have to get out there in the community and look at many factors before committing to a project. That means you have to disqualify a lot of properties in the process, and a lot of those properties will look very attractive at first. Only by looking deeply at every possible angle and by disqualifying those that do not fully measure up can you arrive at the property that is ideal for your needs.

SECRET OF A MILLIONAIRE REAL ESTATE DEVELOPER

7. Your ability to carry a project determines your success or failure.

In December, 2001, I found a two-unit building that I could fix up, renovate, and resell at a hefty profit. The property was located in the Lincoln Park/DePaul area of Chicago, a neighborhood where the average home price exceeds $1 million. I could acquire it for just $280,000—a steal of a deal. There were some obstacles, but this was as sure a bet as I'd ever encountered.

The property had some limitations because it was on a pie-shaped lot. Yet, I knew I could renovate it and sell it as the lowest priced two-flat (two-unit building) in this very exclusive neighborhood. I worked closely with a trusted contractor, someone I'd worked with almost from my first day in real estate development. By the summer of 2002 we had created a very desirable, multiunit dwelling. Each unit had a living room, kitchen, bedroom, and bathroom on one level and a spiral staircase leading up to a master bedroom suite with a private bath on the second level. This was a great property in a great neighborhood selling at a great price.

Although I advertised heavily, the property didn't sell until the summer of 2003.

This time frame was well beyond my expectations: from December of 2001 to July of 2003. I had planned on selling within 8 to 10 months, but the actual amount of time I owned and held the property was 20 months. Yes, I did sell it for a handsome profit, but here's my point. Had I not had the financial reserves to carry the property those extra 10 to 12 months, I'd have risked losing everything—my profit, my hard work, my time, and perhaps the property itself. Remember this story and always, always, always plan on having to carry a property longer than you project. Make sure you have financing adequate to cover expenses long beyond your completion date.

Considerations for Those Already in the Field

For those of you already in the field, the depth of what you are doing has already been determined by your own experience. Where you go or what you want to achieve from this moment on depends entirely on your own drive. Some of you may have reached a level of achievement at which you are satisfied to remain. Others may want to stretch even further.

Some of you may decide to take the "cookie cutter" approach and repeat earlier successes. This isn't necessarily a bad idea. Henry Ford revolutionized the automobile industry, and assured his own fortune, by inventing the automobile production line—a super cookie cutter. That approach was applied to real estate in a place called Levittown on New York's Long Island.

A real estate developer by the name of William Leavitt realized that GIs returning from World War II would face a housing shortage of enormous proportions. To meet that need, and to assure his own fortune, he applied the assembly line concept to housing construction. Using a limited number of housing plans, materials, and techniques that could be applied repeatedly, he created a community of small, detached, and most importantly affordable single-family houses. Larger than a traditional neighborhood, this was a true suburb as we understand the term today. These folks lived in a very real community.

What really made the community different was the fact that it was brand new and had been created from the ground up virtually overnight. And local history would be made by its first inhabitants, who were at first renters and then later because homeowners. Leavitt took a lot of flack from real estate developers, critics, and the media, but his development was a tremendous success. His approach was the right approach, at least for Leavitt, his family, his company, and the happy homeowners of Levittown.

Others of you may take a more adventurous path and strike out for new territory in real estate development. That's fine, too, provided you realize the dangers inherent in new and untested concepts. Of course, at one time Levittown was a bold, controversial, and untested concept. My point is simply that there are many pathways to becoming a millionaire real estate developer. One of the real secrets is to find the best path for you.

Another vital consideration is money. Money is the lifeblood of real estate, as it is with all business endeavors.

SECRET OF A MILLIONAIRE REAL ESTATE DEVELOPER

8. Have a continuous supply of ready money.

Note that modifier "continuous." That's the real secret of the secret. It means developing sources of financing so that you can acquire money whenever you need it, not just for the project at hand. That means developing strong relationships with financing institutions and with the people there who have the power to say "yes" to your proposal. It's a never-ending job and an essential one.

Over the years, we've seen a massive change in the nation's banking system. Many of us can remember the day of the friendly neighborhood bank and the smiling banker who knew you, your family, and your financial condition. Those banks have mostly been replaced by large institutions, and many of those are being replaced by even larger institutions. Lending relationships developed over the years can change overnight. That's why you have to keep working at it. Without those strong relationships you might not get the money you need or you might not get it when you need it or at the most favorable rates.

Please note the following. It's important to maintain good existing financial relationships, *but it's equally important to develop new ones*. Be flexible and adapt to the inevitable changes in your local market and know that more changes are on the way. I'm very loyal to the lending institutions and the people in them who have helped me over the years. I also know that a merger, an acquisition, a transfer, or a promotion could end a given relationship in an instant. I've found throughout my career that by developing new contacts at new banks I always have sources of funding when I need them. And, fortunately, I always need them.

Zoning is another consideration that affects the old pro as well as the novice. Cities are always changing zoning ordinances, sometimes in your favor and sometimes not. Furthermore, a neighborhood's zone may not change, but the allowable use of property within the zone still might change. Height restrictions may go into effect where they have not been used before. Densities may change or items that affect density, such as parking requirements, can change with alarming speed.

Just because you've built before and your projects have sailed through the process relatively unscathed doesn't mean you can automatically repeat the process. City officials change as do neighborhood civic groups, neighborhoods, and neighborhood attitudes towards real estate development.

I've seen many changes take place in the past ten years in Chicago. During the 1994–2004 decade, the city was part of one of the nation's largest development booms. That's been good for the city and very good for me, but increased development has brought, well, new developments. Restrictions were placed on many communities. It seemed that, block by block, neighborhood groups were petitioning their aldermen to put limits on new real estate development. For example, "overlay districts" began to appear on the city zoning map. These districts imposed new demands on developers such as height restrictions or new parking requirements.

Now that we have so many of these overlay districts, the City of Chicago is currently (2004) having to completely rezone itself. Much of this effort was dictated by citizens who demanded that the local government deal with the incredible demand for real estate within the city. Things always change. A successful real estate professional stays on top of such situations, continuously reeducates himself or herself, and adapts as necessary to succeed.

We've heard a lot about the incredible losses people invested in the stock market suffered during 2000–2003. Many of those losses were incurred by young people who had begun investing when the market was rolling. They'd known nothing other than success and ever-increasing returns on their investments. When the market took a nosedive, as it inevitably must, they were not only wiped out, they were shell-shocked. Well, there are boom and bust times in real estate, too. Sure, to my mind, it's the safest, most sure, and certainly the most fun pathway to great wealth, but even considering the industry's long-term stability, there are ups and downs. You have to be prepared to handle both.

In many of my lectures, seminars, articles, and books, I discuss economic trends. One particular observation of mine is often quoted. I have noticed that the nation's economic cycles have tended to follow the same pattern over the past 100 years. The beginning of every decade is the beginning of a recession or depression that lasts through the fourth year of the decade at which time a recovery appears. The recovery usually lasts through the eighth or ninth year, and then a decline appears to drag us into the next recession. This is the Mark B. Weiss economic theory. Remember it!

If you trace each decade you will see my theory unfold for yourself. Go back 100 years. Remember the term "the gay '90s?" Those were the 1890s that lead to the depression of 1900. Remember the roaring '20s that lead to the great depression in the 1930s. Remember the 1980s when Gordon Gecko, played by Michael Douglas in *Wall Street,* proclaimed "greed is good"? That led to the stock market crash in October of 1987 and the banks closing and the recession of the early 1990s and, of course, the tech wreck that ushered in the new millennium. Then, 9/11 hit and the markets took another nosedive. This book will be published in the fall of 2004, and, if my economic theory and observations hold through, we should expand the economy through 2008 at least. But watch out for 2009 and 2010.

What does history tell us? If we're willing to learn, we can see that every strong recession started by an economic downturn in the eight, ninth, or tenth year of a given decade. Boom times begin in the fourth year and generally last until the seventh or eighth. That's the way the economy works. We go from boom to bust to boom, from recovery to recession to recovery. If you're building during that fourth-year to eighth-year period, expect the market to taper off as you move into the ninth and tenth year. That's no reason to stop real estate development. I'm certainly not, but I am taking the business cycles into account and planning my projects, deadlines, and my financing accordingly. For example, if I'm building a property for sale and it's scheduled for completion in that tenth year, I'm not going to cancel the project. I just realize that I might have to earn rental income from it until the economy turns around. I will adjust my plans to fit those needs and still manage to come out ahead. In the long run, I'll come out way ahead.

Being able, willing, and prepared to adapt to an ever-changing environment is one of the keys to success in real estate development.

Pros and Cons of Real Estate Development

I could build a list a couple of chapters long on this subject, but two would dominate that list and I'll just mention those. You'll discover the others throughout this book. The biggest con is that we developers, all of us, could lose a lot of money. That's as inevitable and as predictable as sunrise and sunset. If you get involved in real estate development, then you could lose a lot of money.

The biggest pro is that we developers can make a lot money. The savvy ones, the men and women who learn and apply the secrets of a millionaire real estate developer, focus their attention on the wonderful and dramatic positive side of this business. They know they'll face the con side of real estate, but they're also confident, and even excited, in knowing that they'll come out on the pro side of things. They do very well, very well indeed.

Secrets from the Peak

I'm not the only real estate expert around. I know a lot of very talented, very experienced, and very knowledgeable real estate professionals who are willing to share some of the wealth of their wisdom. You'll find these bits of wisdom at the end of many chapters in this book. They provide other views from different perspectives. Here are eleven secrets from Michael Zucker of Peak Construction LLC in Chicago.

1. Hire a good architect.
2. Hire a good attorney.
3. Expect scheduling errors.
4. Set a realistic schedule.
5. Have a solid exit strategy.
6. Use reputable contractors with the right insurance.
7. Research other developers to see what makes them successful.
8. Visit open houses.
9. Don't skimp on quality.
10. Have a strong customer service program/warrantee program.
11. Make sure budget is well thought out especially for soft costs.

Success Strategies:
Self-Evaluation—Is This for You?

He who knows others is clever, but he who knows himself is enlightened.

Lao Tzu

Understand the Business Before You Join the Business

You are the only one who can evaluate whether you have the time, energy, focus, and drive to become a millionaire real estate developer, but let me give you a few important considerations to help you make that decision. Developing real estate is a full-time job. You may undertake some development projects on a part-time basis, but full time or part time I promise that a real estate career will take more time than you initially think. Whether you're thinking of moving into real estate or of enhancing your existing career in the industry, real estate development will always take more time and cost more money than you have budgeted. That's a fact that comes with the territory. Once you know it and accept it, you can plan to work your way around those obstacles and move on to increasing levels of success.

Forget what you may have read about or heard in real-estate seminars on "how you can make big money in real estate part time" or "buy real estate with no money down." Those claims may sell seminars, but they don't move real estate. When you hire contractors, you have to meet with them before, during, and after the process. You have to meet with representatives of city zoning departments, architects, bankers, accountants, your lawyer, perhaps your doctor, and in Oklahoma and parts of the Southwest maybe even a few Indian chiefs. Conventional business meetings take a tremendous amount of time during the standard 9 to 5 workday. You'll find, too, that as a developer and your own boss, there's no such thing as a 9 to 5 workday. Are you able to handle that? If you're starting out part time, will you be able to get away from your full-time job to meet the commitments of your new career? If you're going at it full time, how will the time devoted to business affect your family life, spiritual and personal growth, and the basic human need for "downtime."

While writing this book, I am working with someone interested in becoming a new developer. His motivation is to augment his job with one of Chicago's largest banks by creating a new income stream through real estate development. Fortunately, he will be receiving money from the sale of a multiunit apartment building that he and his father own. Jim is working on two fronts. First, he continues working at his regular job. Second, during the day, our real estate office is sending, faxing, and e-mailing different properties he considers on two levels. Level one is to reinvest money from his sale of his apartment building. Level two is to find an ideal property to begin his career as a real estate developer.

The first obstacle we have to overcome is setting up appointments for him to view properties. Often he has to take time from work, or he has to meet with us after work to inspect the properties. The difficulties are his inability to leave work early and inability to take advantage of sudden opportunities when they come up on the market. When real estate comes up for sale, because it's a competitive buying environment, things can happen remarkably fast. When a development opportunity comes up, people need to make their offers and take advantage of the transactions. To delay when you need to act is to forfeit opportunity. In Jim's case, we can't get there fast enough because of the time constraints related to his work. One of the items that he is looking to do is acquire a property for renovation. The diligence involved in meeting with the professionals will require him to leave his office on more and more occasions as his new career grows. His employer expects his focus to be 100 percent at work and rightly so. Sooner or later something has to give. He'll have to make a choice between his job and his ability to get the real estate that he wants.

So, how do you dance in two places at once? It's a difficult challenge and not all people are up to it. Of course, those with the millionaire real estate development mindset actually revel in the challenges our business presents. As The Bible tells us, it's impossible to serve two masters equally well. One or the other, or more likely, both will suffer. That's not to say you can't have a successful real estate career and a regular job at the same time. For the reader who hasn't given up his or her day job, you can still be a weekend warrior in real estate. You just have to plan your opportunities around a more limited time frame and undertake challenges that are more manageable. People do this all the time.

When I was in graduate school, the dean of our college had a profitable weekend hobby. He and his son would buy small multiunit buildings in the suburbs just north of Chicago. They would buy a small building and on the weekends enjoy father-and-son time fixing and renovating the building. They'd turn around and sell the real estate for a tidy profit. Their time frame was based on investing a year to buy it, fix it, and sell it. Certainly they accomplished more than just a profit because the time that they spent together was memorable and invaluable. That shared time earned them additional thousands of dollars each year. They also could take pride in accomplishment and in learning more about the real estate industry from their experiences.

That's a sound way to begin a career as a real estate developer. Realize that you are going to have to take away a certain amount of time from your 9 to 5 job commitment. You have to have that flexibility either by using sick days, vacation days, or just additional time off to get out of the office until you can really launch a full-time career. If you're serious about becoming a millionaire real estate developer, you have to find ways to make this happen. Time really is money, and that's especially true in real estate.

Be creative, but be honest. Robbing time from your current employer to fund a new job is not only unethical, it's just no way to build a firm foundation for that new career. The pull between handling two careers at the same time creates stress, and that stress doesn't go away when you move into real estate development full time. Before you make the commitment to this business, I recommend you invest a lot of time in serious self-evaluation. Much of your success as a real estate developer will have to do with how you will deal with stress. Having been in the real estate development arena for about 15 years, I can tell you that I have had more than my share of punches in the jaw, kicks in the head, slaps on the face, and many sleepless nights from unplanned, unexpected, and unwanted events. How do you cope with that? We all go to our jobs, earn our wages, and experience a certain level of stress from having to meet the expectations of the people who oversee our work. And we all find our own ways to cope with stress.

I have observed that many people are overprogrammed. They simply cannot do the things that they undertake due to their many commitments.

These people suffer from what I have discovered and refer too as activity stress disorder (ASD). I noticed this disorder present among young children whose parents had them overprogrammed with too many activities, one after the other after the other. Even when they played, the children could do so only at "play dates," dates that have a time limit, usually a short time limit. Play, as you know, is a free flow of interactions that allows a person's mind to flow creatively. When certain children could no longer cope with this over-programming, they developed physical disorders: rashes, hair loss, cracked skin, and sleeplessness. Adults can develop these symptoms under ASD as well. When you try to do too much, your physical health suffers and your stress shows itself through physical disorders. If you find yourself with anxiety attacks, pealing or flaking skin, or rashes, listen to these signs. Don't take on more stress than you can handle.

The real estate developer experiences stress in a number of forms. It can come when building permits are denied or in thinking that you are buying a piece of property based on a certain representation only to find that the property isn't exactly as promised. A lender may pull out of a deal or change the financing terms at the last minute. While writing this book, I bought a piece of property. The deal flowed nicely, but on the day before closing, my lender called me with an "Oops, because we didn't underwrite the loan correctly, you have to contribute another 5 percent in real cash to make this deal work." City inspectors may visit your site while you are not there and shut you down because of some violation of the municipal code. The stress during the time it takes to get a permit while the clock on your contract is ticking or while the interest-on-your-money clock is ticking away, eroding your revenue, is enormous. I could fill a couple of hundred more pages with examples, but you get the idea.

How do you deal with all these multiple challenges? My suggestion is to handle it the best way you can. Jog. Exercise. Meditate. Take walks around the block, or take up an engrossing hobby. Find a way to relieve the stress that will always be coming your way. Understand that the unexpected in any new venture is going to rear its ugly head to try to bite you in the most painful manner possible. If you are the type of person who doesn't take these kinds of things personally, looks at them solely as business events, and can see the forest through the trees, you will do just fine in real estate development. And you just might become a millionaire in the process.

How often during rough economic times will you read in the paper about large developers having problems and having to bail out of large projects? The answer is "often." In the years of 2000–2004, there were real estate developments underway that were on the drawing board and in the planning stages in the late 1990s during the boom years. With high hopes and a lot of confidence, construction projects popped up all around the country. Developers with the best of intentions watched sadly, and sometimes in shock, as the market evaporated. By 2004 many buildings and large residential developments were owned by real estate *lenders* because the original developers were not able to pay off their loans.

You can't control everything. Realize that fact and accept it. Only then can you deal with it. You also have to accept the fact that stress is part of the package. How will you deal with things over which you will have no control? How do you handle market trends? What do you do when the economy takes a nose dive? Where do you turn when that same market begins to skyrocket?

I stated this earlier and I will emphasize it again because it is worth repeating. Believe it or not, the worst thing that could happen to you is for you to be successful on your first real estate venture. If you don't have very few bumps in the road on your first venture, if everything goes smoothly, and if those anticipated hassles never materialize, your expectation of the next transaction can be overly optimistic. You'll naturally think that things will go just as smoothly. I will promise you this—they won't.

How will all this affect your behavior? How will you react in your other job, to your family, to your friends, to your children who demand your undivided attention on the weekends and during your free time? These are matters you really need to take into consideration in deciding whether real estate development is the career for you.

Establish Your Career Goals

The great architect who developed the Chicago Plan, Daniel Burnham, said "Make no small plans." Of course, he was a successful businessperson when he said that, and "small" is a relative term. Some ventures that in your future will seem small can be major undertakings for someone just starting out. Initially, a plan that is too big will swallow you alive.

As a real estate developer, lecturer, and writer, I am always finding people who are in way over their heads. Here's one example. Someone who had been for many years a commodities trader at the Chicago Board of Trade had given up his career due to volatility in the commodities market. He began developing condominium projects on Chicago's north side. Areas in Chicago are often referred to as the north side, the south side, and the west side. Lake Michigan is to the east. The north side of the city has always been a development boom area, whereas the south side has been home to many people who would fall into the low-income categories. Although Chicago's south side is along Chicago's lakefront, it just has not been as popular as the north side for real estate development, until recently.

Popularity in real estate brings higher prices, bidding wars, and more demand. Areas such as the south and west sides of Chicago had not experienced an increase in demand, and developers who were north-side guys never ventured south to see what they could earn in new territory. Lines between territories aren't always completely logical. For example, another clear line marking north and south relates to sports. White Sox fans never come north. Cubs fans never go south. The rules change for inter-league play. That may not be logical, but it's a fact.

Nevertheless, sometimes the lines are crossed, and a few north-side developers decide to make the trip south. I remember this former commodities trader. He decided to go south where the prices of buildings were less expensive. He felt the ability to renovate projects was just as easy as on the north side, and thus the return on his investment would be much larger than it would have been staying in the territory he knew so well. This man and his investors committed to buying a number of buildings in the area known as South Shore. Because I have established a large network of contacts by letting people know that I am always looking for real estate opportunities, I got a call one day from a Realtor®. He told me about a great opportunity in one of this guy's buildings. I called a community banker and friend who works on the south side of Chicago. I like to have someone with me who is experienced and knowledgeable on the local scene to help me evaluate any investments I am considering. We agreed that his proposal was worth a look.

When we arrived, the 78-unit building looked like an excellent opportunity. It had new windows, and the brick was power-washed and tuck-pointed. A handsome gate around the property building gave it a stately elegance. As we arrived, the broker and the janitor showed up to take us on a tour of the property. A second younger broker tagged along to learn how to be successful in brokering real estate deals. We were told that the owner was coming too because he wanted to be with us and show us the wonderful work he had done to this building.

The property appeared to be a great value, something I am always looking to buy. Yet once inside the apartments, we saw that they were in deplorable condition. The problem was from tenant abuse, deferred maintenance, a fire, and other mishaps. Many rooms were all gutted. As it was once said about Los Angeles, there was "no *there* there." This developer left his safe harbor and came to an area that he wasn't familiar with on a number of levels. His theory was that he was going to renovate this building by spending money on half the property while the other half would pay him rent. The people who were living in this building had other ideas and decided that they weren't going to pay him rent. The cash flow that he anticipated stopped flowing. He also hadn't crunched his numbers very well. He'd spent all of his real estate development money to own a building that was half gutted and half not paying him rent. That's not what I mean by "careful evaluation and planning."

It gets worse. The tenants he had inherited were heavily involved in underworld drug dealing. His property was the center of criminal enterprise. He couldn't win. Thus he was trying to bail out of the situation. When he appeared at the property, he had a defensive air and didn't know how to admit that he would really take anything to get out of this building. What option other than bank foreclosure did he have? He'd be left with only bad credit and expensive legal bills. The property would be continually surrounded by police officers shouting "come out with your hands up."

He was not ready to face the reality of the problem he'd created. Self-delusion is a common and deadly trap. A few weeks later in thinking about his dilemma, I called him into my office and asked him if I could act as his real estate broker because I knew that with my skills I could help him sell this property at a profit. I asked him, "What do you really need to get out of this deal?" But he was not willing to get off his sinking ship. My experience tells me that he will go down with that ship.

My point in telling you this story is simply this: stay where you know, do what you know, and don't necessarily make big plans before you're ready to take them on. Because a 78-unit building was more than this fellow could handle; the neighborhood was more than this fellow could handle; the com-

---

 SECRET OF A MILLIONAIRE REAL ESTATE DEVELOPER

9. Establish your career goals early.

mitment of time and effort was more than this fellow could make, he has had many sleepless nights. His partners are trying to get their money out of the deal. He won't listen to his own inner voice, and, at some point in the future when the bank forecloses on the real estate, someone else will slip into his shoes. While he is licking his wounds and fretting over his "bad breaks," the new developer may be able to take advantage of his good work and good intentions.

What do you really want to do? How do you want to do financially in a reasonable way? What steps should you take to get there? And, just as important, what steps should you avoid along the way?

The first building that I began renovating as a real estate developer was a three-flat that I lived in with my wife. It was an excellent investment back in the 1990s, and we still own it. We bought this building to live in, hired a general contractor, renovated the owners' unit, lived in it, had our tenants pay our mortgage, and actually had a positive cash flow of a couple hundred bucks in our pocket every month. Our property is certainly worth a lot more today, and the work we did still holds true. We planned carefully and worked hard. It was good work, and the amount of money we have had to reinvest in this property has been minimal over the years. It's been quite a successful real estate development.

This was a project that we did while we were working, and although we weren't neophytes to real estate, it still took twice the amount of time we thought it would take. We also experienced a general contractor who went into bankruptcy and out of business before we could complete the project. We had to finish this job on our own. It was a long, slow process, but we finished it and benefited from the process in the long run. And so it goes. Even though you work harder, invest more time, spend more money, and experience more setbacks than you plan on, you can still come out on top.

Watch what other people are doing, and when they do something right, follow their lead. Look at how they do it. Establish credit at institutions, know where your money is going to come from, and pay a little more for good general contractors and subcontractors rather than always going with the least expensive guy. Every time we have chosen to go with the lowest bidder, he has gone out of business and left us high and dry. Whenever I have worked with an individual or company outside of the handful of contractors that I have used successfully over the years, my rash actions have turned around to bite me in the you know what.

The following statement is extremely important.

👉 **SECRET OF A MILLIONAIRE REAL ESTATE DEVELOPER**

10. Listen to that small, quiet inner voice.

You know best! I have always been sorry for not paying more attention to those inner messages. Today, I listen to my conscience and judgment more than ever before. As time passes and I gain more experience, knowledge, and insight, I find that inner voice is louder and clearer than anytime in the past. It has proven to be an excellent guide in making the right decisions and establishing career goals.

In the long run, and in the short run, too, you will always do better when you are able take on reasonable challenges. Taking on a lofty goal before you're up to that challenge can lead to financial, mental, and emotional disaster. Finding a fixer-upper home, an inexpensive condo in a great area of the city, or a little vacant plot of land that a prefab home can be built on and resold are great ways to begin. They're doable even for people beginning their first development. The solid singles you hit will be much more satisfying than the strike outs trying to hit unattainable homeruns.

It is much more fun to make money than to lose money. Believe me, I've done both. It sounds simple doesn't it, but people often don't look at the reality of the downside, and there's always a downside. They only look at a prospective deal from an optimist's point of view. Millionaire real estate developers are very optimistic people, but they always examine a development from every angle. Learn from their example. Conduct your own study and research and then figure out what is the best course of action. Crunch your own numbers and study what other people do and how they achieve their successes. Continue your studies and let the learning curve boost you into higher and higher levels of accomplishment.

I think that if you set out to do one or two projects per year, you will be setting realistic expectations. The projects that you will try to do will probably be manageable in the sense of a small-scale operation. And that's a great way to begin.

Develop a Five-Year Plan of Action

Here is an easy five-year plan for you to follow if you are looking at real estate development as your career. Take the time to do this right. Every moment you invest in study, planning, and gaining experience pays off in dollars, time, and worries saved in your later years.

Year one. Study the market, look at what real estate developers do, ask questions, attend seminars, visit your local Home Depot to ask the suppliers of materials and equipment their opinions of the downfalls or pitfalls that contractors run into. Interview contractors, attorneys, and other real estate professionals. Seek help in locating properties for development on a reasonable scale to get your career started. Interview bankers and lenders. Establish yourself as a good businessperson so that you can get the lines of credit and construction loans you will need. Set a goal that by the end of the first year you have bought and closed on your first piece of property. Make that commitment and stick to it.

Year two. Complete the renovations, if any, of the property purchased at the end of year one. Sell it, rent it, or refinance it, but complete the project before the end of year two. Take notes during the process so that you have a record of where you have been and where you are at the moment. A journal of your earliest real estate activities will be an important reference tool for years to come. Make a list of items that you would do again. Make another list of projects and events you would prefer to avoid. If you choose to acquire your second piece of real estate development property, make sure you do so only after closing on property number one.

Years three, four, and five. Follow the same process you began in years one and two. When you get to year five, sit down, review your journal, and seriously evaluate your next steps. After succeeding for five years in any business, and real estate development is certainly a business, you should have attained a satisfactory level of achievement and success. It usually takes five years for a business to become profitable. I hope that your adventure into the field of real estate will be more profitable than your initial expectations. Nothing is guaranteed, but it's been my experience over the years that small steps early on lead to big gains down the road.

During your first five years you will make contacts, you will meet people, you will observe opportunities that you will be increasingly better prepared to undertake. Your fear factor will be diminished, and new options will arrive that wouldn't open to you unless you were active in the field. I firmly believe that if you plan carefully and stick to that plan, you will amaze yourself at the level of success you will attain.

Career Change—Part-Time or Full-Time Profession

Your first few real estate development deals may not provide you with a year's salary, and that's another reason for extremely careful planning. If you're holding down a job in another profession and working part time in real estate, you should still earn a number of bonuses for your efforts. Some of these will be financial, but others will be in other areas. You will experience a growing sense of accomplishment, a pride in creating a better life and more secure future, and a feeling of confidence as your expertise grows.

The safe way to venture into the real estate market full time is to have the equivalent of two years' wages saved so that you can devote your time to your new business. Although I am not a proponent of partners in real estate deals or any businesses for that matter, sometimes sharing that risk with another person is an acceptable idea for someone just starting out in the business. It's essential that you know the other person's level of commitment and how willing he or she is to share the responsibilities and risks. The partnership can add more of a burden to your business transactions, or it can lighten the load. Again, studying and planning up front can eliminate a lot of frustration and heartbreak later on. It takes a special kind of group to coordinate a non-jealous equity-driven partnership, but it can be done. You just have to be careful in selecting your partners and in structuring your partnership agreements. Career changes are difficult at best, and real estate is full of incredible challenge and opportunity. Leave nothing to chance.

I have known many people who have entered real estate development unprepared to handle the challenges. Some of them jumped in without a long-term plan. Others started without proper capitalization. Because their growing list of bills outdistanced their not-so-growing list of income-producing properties, they got into big trouble fast. Others partnered up with the wrong people or failed to structure their agreements properly. I know a few who "just knew" that real estate would prove to be the answer to all their problems only to discover they really weren't cut out for the profession. All of these situations, and some of them were tragic, could have been avoided if the people involved had only invested the proper time to consider what they were about to do.

The people I have known who have established themselves well have done quite well. Success in real estate development really boils down to a matter of choice. Do you choose to do things the wrong way and set yourself on a course for guaranteed failure? Or do you follow the lead of those who have gone before and set sail for safe harbors, professional achievement, and financial success?

The Importance of a Long-Term Plan

"The impact of long-term planning depends upon decisions that are made today and not decisions in the future." That quote came from a Certified Commercial Investment Member (CCIM) instructor in a commercial investment course I took in the mid-1980s. It seemed to me so profoundly obvious that I typed the quote on a piece of paper that I keep under the glass on my desk to remind me of the importance of early planning. Millionaire real estate developers "seize the day" because they planned to do so yesterday. Whether you are planning on real estate development as a full-time or part-time endeavor, start that planning right now. Don't put off this essential task. You may want to modify your plan in the future, and that's okay. We are always modifying our plans, but the first step in reaching a goal of any sort is to develop a plan in the beginning.

Here are questions to ask in setting a long-term plan. First, what do you want to accomplish? Second, what is your time frame? Third, can you acquire the resources to accomplish the plan?

Evaluating Your Market

Every market is different. Every person entering that market is different and has different goals, resources, and needs. What you hope to achieve in your market will depend on an incredible variety of items and circumstances, including your budget, the availability of money, your level of knowledge and experience, the quality of your suppliers and associates, your aspirations, time, energy, drive, and so on. Given that, I can still make two very important across-the-board recommendations:

1. Select a specialization.
2. Acquire education, information, resources, and contacts.

Specialization will always keep your development efforts lean and mean. You may prefer building single-family homes, town homes, or shopping centers, or some other kind of real estate. You may also find specialization can be boring at times because of its repetitive nature. Of course, you can say that about any job. Yet, specialization often makes you operate in an expeditious and flawless way. Trying to do too much with too little expertise, know-how, and resources is a surefire way of courting disaster. It's called spreading yourself too thin, and that's no way to become a millionaire real estate developer.

Using the same trading techniques over and over again to accomplish the same goals, dealing with the same attorneys repetitively to accomplish the same goals, dealing with the same architects repetitively to accomplish the same goals, dealing with the same marketplace repetitively to accomplish the same goals will just simply end up making you more money. You will soon be able to write your deals on the back of a matchbook. You'll know where your business comes from, who your buyers are, how to set up your marketing strategy, and how to decorate a model home. A vast amount of knowledge will become so ingrained that you can pull it up from memory whenever needed. You can make better decisions faster because of that vast wealth of information that's stored in your brain and is therefore always on call.

Selecting a specialization is a great way to become a successful real estate developer. I know because I practice what I preach. My area of specialization is vintage renovations. My team takes over a multiunit vintage building. We maintain the shell but replace the guts of the interior and put in modern amenities. We add an in-unit laundry, new kitchens, larger baths, individual heat and air-conditioning, and other improvements. We know how to deal with the obstacles that existing conditions present. And we're quite good at it. Others developers like taking vacant land or tearing down the existing structure and building up new structures. Our team works more rapidly with a building that is already standing. This is one of the great benefits of real estate development. There are so many good choices that everyone can find his or her own special niche.

It is important to determine what you like and what is best for your long-term career goals. No one thing is best for everyone. By knowing your market and developing your area of expertise, your specialty will help to accomplish the worthy goal of making more money easily and quickly.

Network. Network. Network! Get out into the marketplace often. Put your finger on the pulse of your community. I am one who is a proponent of learning by doing. Unless you are out there doing business, everything becomes very abstract. If you are not out there putting money on the line, walk-

---

 SECRET OF A MILLIONAIRE REAL ESTATE DEVELOPER

11. Network.

---

ing into buildings, picking out tile, interviewing attorneys, spending time in meetings, attending local Realtor and builder club seminars, you will never learn this business. You have to push yourself to sit in programs where you may not initially understand the terminology and jargon. You'll have to pick it all up. You must buy books and then read, study, and understand them. Walk into construction sites and talk to contractors on the job to find out what and how things get done. It's part of the job, and you just have to do it. I find that picking up knew knowledge is one of the more satisfactory and rewarding benefits of a career in real estate.

Those investments will all pay off in due time. And in due time you will discover that along the way you have become a millionaire real estate developer.

Linda's Secrets

1. Assemble a great team of the best: architects, brokers, attorneys, and contractors. It's critical that all the players have the same spirit, integrity, and level of expertise.
2. Be the most knowledgeable about your community in which you're building. Be involved in the political arena.
3. Gain an understanding of what the market needs, not necessarily what you like or have been building. Know what you need to supply to the market. Create a unique product that the market can absorb.
4. A good developer must be well-funded. There are always "bumps in the road" that are unforeseen.
5. Limit the number of investors in a project, especially large multiunit developments. Having too many investors involved compromises the integrity of a project.
6. A good developer must follow up, especially after the closing. It's the little things that make the big impressions. Return all the clients' calls and respond to their needs and concerns. A developer who wants a long career will develop a following by word-of-mouth from a lot of satisfied customers sooner than you would expect.
7. Integrity, dependability, consistency are huge characteristics to cultivate.
8. Be ambitious. Have a get it done attitude with a sense of urgency.
9. A developer must be close enough to the market to make smart acquisitions. That is why we so often see out-of-town developers get killed!
10. Have pride in your workmanship. Buyers want to believe that their developer wants the best for them *and* himself or herself.

Linda Levin is a Realtor in Chicago. As a sales agent, Linda has represented developers in the sale of property since 1988.

Legal

What the large print giveth, the small print taketh away.

Anonymous

A millionaire real estate developer is by definition a team leader. A developer is the leader of a skilled, talented, and experienced group of professionals who are some of the best in their respective fields. The visual image of King Arthur and his Knights of the Round Table is a dramatic, but appropriate illustration. The king, that's you, sits at the only position of prominence and is the center of attention. All the other knights, your suppliers, occupy equal stations around you. All are important. Each has specific and necessary skills that come into play as they are needed. Different members of the team take the lead whenever their specific skills require it, but nobody outranks the king.

The key members of a complete team are: attorney, financial advisor, accountant, construction/maintenance personnel, influencers, and contacts. Of course, a "member" may actually be several persons or a company, but regardless of who or how many are involved, you must make sure these team positions are filled.

A lot of the advice and techniques I offer in this chapter apply to finding a good financial advisor, an accountant, construction/maintenance personnel, influencers, and contacts. When looking for anyone with whom to conduct business, you'll want to ask around, get references, contact professional organizations, conduct interviews, and so on. So, I'll not repeat myself that much in the following chapters, hoping that you realize the advice in Chapter 3 flows through Chapter 7.

I'm leading off with the legal aspects because America today is such a litigious society. Everybody seems to be suing everybody else for reasons that range from the necessary and obvious to the frivolous and embarrassing. Trust me now or learn from bitter experience later on. You need a good lawyer, a very good lawyer, and you'd be crazy to wait until you've "made it" to start working with one. Here's what to look for in a lawyer and how to go about looking.

The Three Key Attributes of a Great Attorney

A great attorney will have a lot of positive characteristics, but I think three are essential. You want more, of course, but without these key attributes the others will be virtually worthless. What are they?

1. Knowledge of the law
2. A good local reputation
3. Solid real estate experience

Knowledge of the Law

This sounds obvious, but I advise you to check out just how much your attorney knows about the law. There's an old joke about wondering whether the surgeon who is about to open you up was an A, B, C, or remedial student. It's a good and legitimate question. Professionals all have nice diplomas beautifully mounted on their walls, but what do those diplomas really represent? I've known some brilliant lawyers in my time, and I've run into my share of knuckleheads. You can't always tell which is which by the framed certificates on the wall, the price of the three-piece suit, or the number of lackies who follow when he or she walks into a room.

It's a given that just about any professional in a business laden with technical and legal terminology, insider jargon, and especially the language of the law can talk rings around someone with just a layman's experience. You don't have to become a lawyer just to talk to a lawyer. One of the best weapons of understanding in your arsenal is to know your own business. Be so well-educated and up to date on real estate development that he or she can't double-talk you when you say "put that in plain English, please." Ask probing questions and demand answers that you can easily understand. Don't be shy about asking repeatedly until you get a firm grasp on the matter. Any lawyer who can't or won't provide that simple service is not one you want on your team anyway.

Don't be fooled by a fancy office, a large staff, or hourly rates that are approaching near-earth orbit. An attorney can have all that and still be a legal also-ran. Appearances really can be deceiving. Real estate developers are not immune to this syndrome, by the way. I once encountered an aggressive young attorney who began expounding (pontificating, really) as to how he brought in new corporate business. He regaled me with vivid descriptions of his palatial offices, his large staff, the four-color multipage brochure he mailed to prospective clients, and the entourage he brought with him to make his presentations. I smiled, nodded, and was polite, but what kept hitting me throughout his "speech" was the fact that he never once mentioned his knowledge of the law. For him business was all about show and had very little to do with genuine customer service. You have to ask a lot of questions. If you're not satisfied with the answers, it's your right and your obligation to continue looking for the best attorney you can find.

 **SECRET OF A MILLIONAIRE REAL ESTATE DEVELOPER**

12. You must be the leader.

Regardless of the professionals you have on your team, you lead the charge. Have your lawyers do what you want them to do. I like having knowledgeable professionals around me, but they must do what I say and when. It's not a matter of my looking for them to support my opinion. But if I need a contract drawn up, I need it now, not later. And I need it perfectly executed. After a contract is accepted, it is almost always subject to attorney review for clean up of terms and conditions anyway. So I need an attorney who is ready and able to make those changes whenever they're needed.

Sometimes You Have to Fire Members of Your Team

I don't like reinventing the wheel. I like one party who knows how I like to buy and sell property so I don't have to explain or justify my habits, terms, and conditions to the new kid on the block every time I make a deal. My first active attorney handled a number of transactions with me over time and then one day became greedy. His bill was excessive for the work he did not do. I say did *not* do, because although we hadn't completed the transaction, I received a huge bill. I sent the bill back and stopped using him; I couldn't trust him any longer.

I then called another attorney to take over this man's work, and he and I worked well together for many years. Over eight to ten years we did more than 100 transactions. Over time his fee keep creeping up, and when I would question the fee increases, he would answer me in a snide way, "The fee can always get higher." That's not what I consider a thoughtful answer.

I even took his son-in-law in on a couple of deals as a small partner. This fellow was a teacher and apparently did not make a great living. He had many kids too, so when his father-in-law asked if the son-in-law could share in the profits, I agreed. The son-in-law, although a small partner, made out great. But my lawyer kept sneaking in fee increases over time for conventional work, not unusual or complex transactions.

The attorney also cost me a few deals because he worked at perfecting a contract from the get go. We all know that there is a give and take anyway, and that whatever I present will be countered, etc. But this man cost me deals because he dragged his feet trying to create the perfect contract. Often by the time he had something for me, the property was gone. Although his reputation was disputable, he did okay for me during my formative years as a developer and I made money, but over time he was costing me money by losing deals and in the unnecessary fees I had to pay. The last straw was during a refinance of four properties. I consulted the attorney's paralegal, his wife, to get the documents prepared for the refinance. Frankly we spent more time than we should have, but the attorney himself had little to no time invested in the refinance.

I asked that my attorney schedule the closing at the title company. My attorney virtually lived at the title company anyway because he performed hundreds of closings each year. He was there when the funding arrived. For those who don't know what a refinance involves, it's actually taking out a new loan to replace the existing loan. Other than signing documents, the money comes in and then goes to pay off the old lender. When I reviewed the closing statement, my dear loyal attorney had a fee for himself on each loan statement. The fee was obscene just because it was on the statement. The amount certainly exceeded the amount this man was entitled to receive. That was our last transaction. I was through. I don't like being taken advantage of and neither should you. This brings us to our next topic.

Reputation

If someone doesn't have a good local reputation, there's got to be a reason and it's probably not a good one. I don't care if your candidate appears as a commentator on top-rated cable network news programs, or if his or her photo makes the national periodicals, or if this person is regularly called to Washington, D.C., to confer with the powers that be. What do the locals think? And why?

Remember that even the best people make enemies. People gossip, and untrue stories can circulate as gospel truth. It's important to ask a lot of people. Get different opinions from a variety of people in diverse businesses. Do not base your decision on who is getting a lot of positive local "press" either. I can't remember how many times I've read glowing stories or features about a local attorney in which he or she is made to appear a virtual saint, a business leader of immense proportions, and perhaps the next Chief Justice just weeks before that attorney declared bankruptcy, was indicted for a high crime, or absconded to Bermuda with the company piggy bank.

There's an unscientific rule I use when evaluating high-powered talent. Ask around and find out whether or not this lawyer (accountant, banker, influencer, etc.) returns his or her phone calls. That tells you a lot about this person's ego, business skills, and willingness to work for a client.

Your local chamber of commerce, better business bureau, bar association, and other professional groups are good sources of information. You may not get specific recommendations, but if there's a trend in those who go unmentioned, you still have valuable information. Again, talk to people, a lot of people. Pretty soon you'll have a short list of likely candidates you can personally screen.

Meet with the attorney or the lead attorney for real estate if you're interviewing a firm. Too often I've seen or even experienced situations in which a prospective client is "wined and dined" by the top people in the company only to learn later that the junior trainees are doing all the real work. Meet and get an impression of the people who will actually be running the plays on your team. Who knows, even though you may not be impressed by all the wining and dining, you might discover that those junior trainees are an aggressive, hardworking, dedicated group of fire-breathers.

This is a rough guideline, but unless you're dealing in projects budgeted at a million dollars or more, you probably won't need to hire a large legal firm with a huge support staff. Your needs just won't require that depth of service. You'd be paying for a lot of people, paper, and processes that you really don't need. Individuals just beginning in real estate development should look for what I call a "downtown" attorney. That's someone who may or may not have an office downtown but who has downtown connections. He or she knows the people at city hall, the financial wheelers and dealers, and the contacts you need to "grease the wheels" of your project. This is someone who can shepherd you through those early, trying days and help hone your skills, abilities, and experiences as a developer.

Take the responsibility to conduct some of your own research, especially in the latter stages. Remember, these folks may be your lawyers, but it's your business and ultimately it's your fortune and your reputation on the line.

Real Estate Savvy

As I write this, a very high-profile attorney is representing two very high-profile clients in two controversial cases. One involves a multiple murder and the other charges of abuse by a rock star. I don't know the attorney, but he has a very good reputation according to the newspapers, magazines, and broadcast news programs. I don't know that I'd hire him to be my business attorney, though. Sure, if the authorities came knocking on my door and started asking about the Lindbergh kidnapping, a Brinks job, or the location of the missing crown jewels, I'd be looking up his phone number ASAP. But I still don't think I'd let him handle my real estate business.

The legal side of real estate development is a very specialized arena. A terrific attorney in criminal or corporate law may be out of his or her league in handling real estate development matters. Just ask for a rundown of the individual's or the firm's real estate experience. Let me stress the fact that real estate law is complex, difficult, and ever-changing. A successful developer doesn't have the time to learn the law, and a busy entrepreneur certainly doesn't have the time to keep up with the constantly changing nature of real estate law and regulation. You need professionals who can and will do that for you, and those professionals had better know what they're doing. Their lack of expertise could cost you a lot more than legal fees. Ignorance of the law is no excuse, and neither is "But my lawyer told me . . ." If you cross the line, even unknowingly, you could find yourself and your project in a painful and embarrassing lawsuit, pilloried in the press, appearing before government tribunals, or even being put out of business.

While writing this book, I purchased a six-unit investment property and throughout that time we were preparing for closing, I heard from both my attorney and the Realtor involved in the transaction that the seller's attorney was impossible to reach and when contacted he was never prepared. This was frustrating for all parties involved. I met this man, a flamboyant figure, for the first time at the closing. He had not ordered a survey, and that responsibility fell on the seller's Realtor. Just one week before closing he had not gotten a water certification that the City of Chicago required prior to closing. Other standard items were not ready when the closing date arrived. At the closing, this man unleashed an outburst at the seller's Realtor over a minor "nonissue" matter. He really showed his colors there. After the closing, the sellers were noticeably embarrassed by this man's behavior and actually asked my attorney for his card so they could hire him for future transactions.

When I arrived back at my office, one of my salesmen approached me and said "So, I heard that you had a closing this morning with my director." I asked what he was talking about. It turns out that the seller's attorney was actually a community college drama director, and my agent was in many of his plays over the years. This man was only a "part-time" (a very part-time) lawyer. No wonder he was not prepared. Now it made sense. I am sure the sellers hired him for his low fee.

> *"A low fee does not a real estate attorney make."*
>
> Mark B. Weiss

Remember my quote. Be sure you surround yourself with trained professionals that you can work with.

Real estate law and regulation varies from state to state and even from community to community. You'll need someone who is up to speed in your specific market. The differences may not be significant and may be easily understood, but tiny differences can have major consequences. Be aware that if your business interests cross state lines, and depending on the state, you may encounter enormous differences. I met a young lawyer who had graduated from law school in Georgia. He'd earned good grades and was looking forward to getting started on a successful career. The young man had married a young woman from Louisiana who had a lot of family and friends in "The Bayou State," so he decided to set up shop there. He told me that Louisiana operated under the Napoleonic Code. Before setting up shop, he had to learn a set of laws unlike any other in the United States, certainly a different set than those under which he was trained. None of this should discourage you from conducting business anywhere in the United States. Just be aware that there are differences, often subtle ones, that may have a dramatic impact on the success of your real estate developments. A good lawyer or legal team will know how to shoulder that burden for you.

I recommend that your attorney have a good understanding of accounting as it applies to real estate. You don't want your lawyer keeping your books, but you do want a second "set of eyes" looking over your financial shoulder. Much of today's litigation involves the financial side of the business, and you don't want your attorney playing catch up while the bailiff is shouting "order in the court." The attorney doesn't have to be an expert, but he or she should have a solid foundation of knowledge and be able to communicate with your accountant without the aid of an interpreter and vice versa. Remember, every deal you do requires you pay taxes, capital gains, or ordinary income as well as transfer taxes and more. Your attorney should be aware of your tax requirements and address them in setting forth your transaction.

Build a Harmonious Relationship

Relationship is a key word that means more than just working with someone. A feeling of mutual trust between lawyer and developer is key to a successful relationship. You don't have to be brothers or sisters, belong to the same civic club, or go bowling together on weekends. You really don't even have to like each other that much. But there should be a bond of trust.

The relationship should also be a comfortable one, and this can get tricky. Lawyers, especially trial lawyers, by their nature have to employ intimidation tactics at times. Some employ them all the time, even with their clients. It's easy to fall prey to these techniques. Lawyers are like doctors, computer geeks, priests, and rabbis. They all have their own mystical language that is not accessible by we mere mortals. That's fine. Let them have their language, rituals, and mysteries. Just remember that as the client you are the boss. You call the shots, make the decisions, pay the bills, and ultimately are responsible under the law for your actions. Each of you had better be comfortable with that reality and act accordingly. Got that, boss?

What should a developer expect from a good attorney? Many things, but among them are the comfortable and trustworthy relationship just mentioned. Your attorney should respond to your phone calls or e-mails promptly, just as you'd expect from any supplier. Again, despite the fancy offices and legalese he or she tosses about, the attorney is in your hire. Never forget that. You want someone who will take the appropriate time to meet with you whenever necessary to provide whatever services are necessary. You need an individual who is willing to invest the time to make sure every *i* is dotted and every *t* is crossed. Your attorney should be open to answer any questions you have about billing—promptly, in detail, and without rancor.

Don't underestimate the importance of harmony in a lawyer/client relationship. I don't mean the kind of lotus-eating harmony New Agers seek with the universal whachamacallit. I mean a working relationship that is as free as possible of hassles, squabbles, and ruffled feathers. You just don't have time for that. I'm not saying that you have to make a lot of chit chat or pat each other on the back every time one of you enters the room, but your professional relationship should also be an easygoing one for each of you. Tension or just a slight feeling of discomfort could prevent either party from bringing up an important topic. Lack of effective communication always comes back to bite you.

Regardless of an attorney's skill or reputation, if the relationship lacks harmony, it probably won't work in the long run. I recommend that you seek counsel elsewhere. This may be more important than many of you realize. Remember, you'll be working closely on very important and often stressful situations. You'll be providing this other person or company a lot of very private and privileged business information. You have to be comfortable with that. Otherwise, you might hold back some bit of vital information or insight and legally shoot yourself in the foot. Hey, just take a look at your local telephone yellow pages. I don't care where you live, it's packed with ads for lawyers. Surely there's one in all those pages with whom you can establish a great rapport.

 SECRET OF A MILLIONAIRE REAL ESTATE DEVELOPER

13. Hire the best legal minds you can afford.

And you can afford more than you think. I've seen too many developers try to skate by this reality. They trim their budget by hiring some lawyer off the street, an inexperienced kid right out of school, or a cousin or brother-in-law who took some law courses in college. That's really skating on thin ice. Believe me. Your lawyer's lack of experience can cost you a fortune. It can even put you out of business. The risk just isn't worth the alleged savings.

How to Work with Your Attorney

Think of your relationship with your attorney as a true partnership, but one in which you are the boss. By "boss" I don't mean a dictatorial despot bellowing petty orders and demanding total and unquestioning allegiance. Your attorney has a business to run also, and he or she has other valuable clients. Respect is a two-way street. Each of you should give as good as you get.

I'm a strong believer in courtesy. I often note that "please" and "thank you" are two of the most valuable and least used forms of compensation in U.S. business. Even in the sometimes rough-and-tumble world of real estate development, there's room for politeness. And despite media images, the so-called toughest or meanest SOBs in the business aren't necessarily the most successful in the long run. I'm reminded of a Hollywood western about a tenderfoot who joined a trail drive headed by a tough veteran of the trails. The harsh, and often savage, ways of the trail at first shock the tenderfoot. As the movie progresses he changes his personality to fit his image of the tough cowhand. Towards the end of the film, the trail boss looks at him and says, "You ain't got tough. You just got miserable."

That's no way to live, and it's certainly no way to run a business or maintain a healthy relationship. Your attorney should be willing to meet with you person-to-person periodically. Some information you just don't want to transmit over the telephone, fax machine, or through e-mail. Besides, face-to-face meetings from time to time, even if it's just a business lunch, help cement the relationship and keep things running smoothly when those stressful times arrive.

As with any relationship, it is imperative that you handle your responsibilities, too. Yes, you, the boss, have responsibilities to your lawyer. You have a responsibility to be open and honest. This is a privileged relationship and there's no reason to withhold vital information from a trusted person working on your behalf. You have a responsibility to be prepared for your meetings and any appearances, such as presentations to bankers or business personnel, government bodies, or in court. If you're supposed to bring documents or materials to a meeting, then be sure to bring them. That's especially true if your attorney's office is to provide certain legal services. For example, if you need something notarized, be sure to bring proof that you're who you say you are. Don't laugh. Many a productive meeting has been busted up because the client forgot the wallet with his or her ID in it.

Here's a thought. Before any meeting, call your attorney and ask for a list of the materials you should bring along. You'll be prepared. Neither of you will waste the other's time, and the meeting should sail along without hitting any troubled waters caused by your lack of preparedness. Such a call might also jog the memory of your attorney who will make doubly sure that he's prepared, too.

I've mentioned the term *legalese.* That's a popular word for all the terms and jargon used by the legal profession that we common folks just don't understand, don't have time to understand, and really don't want to understand. Well, a millionaire real estate developer has to understand at least the concepts. You don't have to know the jargon, but you do have to understand the meaning of the papers you're signing, the agreements you're making, and the laws you're (hopefully) following. Ask for definitions in plain English. Ask until you get the information you need presented in a manner that you can understand. This is essential. Never sign a document or make an agreement containing a word, phrase, sentence, paragraph, or page that you do not fully understand. This is a key responsibility of your attorney, but it is also a key responsibility of the client (you) to ask for, yes demand, the information you need.

Other Concerns

There are a number of legal and legal-related matters a millionaire real estate developer faces and must handle. To my mind, the following are the major considerations.

Charges and Billing

Before hiring a lawyer, or any supplier, get a detailed list of all charges and how they will be billed. That knowledge cannot only make a real difference in your decision to hire, it can have a real impact on your monthly profitability. For example, does or how does the attorney charge for telephone calls. Some charge nothing for a basic "how are things going" type call. Others charge for such calls by the minute, and others charge in 15-minute increments regardless of the length of the call. Make four phone calls and even if they're less than a minute each, you're suddenly paying for an hour of an attorney's time. You'd be amazed at how fast that can add up.

If you have a question about a bill or a charge, then by all means ask. Get clarification. You might be satisfied with the answer. They might discover an error in their bookkeeping. You both may end up negotiating a satisfactory compromise. Honest lawyers and legal firms will be open and upfront and will want to quickly clear up any possible misunderstandings. If you get a round of dissatisfying answers or "tap dancing" from their accounting department, you have a problem far more serious than one charge on your hands. It's time to start looking around for new legal representation.

Don't be shy about negotiating either. Negotiation is an essential skill for the millionaire real estate developer, and there's no reason you should draw a line at your attorney's office. (See Chapter 10 for a few negotiating tips.) If you think the fees and charges are too high, say so. See if you can work out some type of mutually comfortable arrangement. As with any negotiation, it's important that each side come away with something. Don't try to "hammer" your lawyer just for the pleasure of getting a lower fee. Such tactics might bring a bit of temporary pleasure, but they can backfire in the long run. When you pick the pocket of the person on your side, he or she doesn't remain on your side very long.

Suing for Malpractice

If you've done your homework, checked out all the references thoroughly, and interviewed carefully, malpractice should be one of the least of your concerns. Yet, it happens. It's a matter you should approach carefully, fully prepared, and without emotion. That last one is important. It's easy to let anger over a legal situation get the better of you. Don't. Cool down. Marshal your facts and figures. Evaluate them carefully and proceed only if you really think you have a serious case.

I think most of the malpractice cases I've seen could have been avoided had both parties made a serious effort all along to simply speak to each other. My attitude is that if you have a question, pick up the phone, make a call, and get the answer. Too many people allow a situation to fester until the only

---

☞ **SECRET OF A MILLIONAIRE REAL ESTATE DEVELOPER**

14. Don't waste time, money, and emotion on unnecessary "payback" through lawsuits or any other means.

---

apparent recourse is to use the legal system. Well, that system is there and I'm glad it's in place, but I'll try my best to prevent those kinds of situations from coming up in the first place. I urge you to adopt this policy. As a millionaire real estate developer, you'll just have too much else to do. Having been involved in litigation, I can tell you, in the long run no one wins.

Protect the Lawyer/Client Privilege

This is one of your most serious responsibilities because the privilege is one of the foundations of our legal systems and one of your greatest assets. In our system, we place a premium on privacy. Therefore communication between a lawyer and his or her client is considered privileged. It's supposed to stay between the two parties. The police, the sheriff, the federal authorities, even the courts are prohibited from violating that privilege. By law whatever is communicated between you and your lawyer stays between you and your lawyer. Your lawyer, and his or her staff, is also bound by this privilege. They can't be compelled to reveal confidential communications relating to your business.

It is possible to lose this privilege. Privileged communication must remain strictly between you and your legal representation. If a third party is privy to the communication, all bets are off. For example, let's say you discuss matters in a meeting with your attorney and you wish all that information to remain confidential. Well and good, unless there's a third party in the room or on the phone or hooked up to the video conferencing equipment. This third party might be your accountant, a financial advisor, a counselor, or some other involved person. That third party is not bound by the lawyer/client privilege even if the meeting takes place in your lawyer's conference room.

The way around this is simple. Just don't discuss privileged information with any third party. That's easier said than done. If you're rolling along in a meeting, it's easy to forget yourself and start discussing confidential matters. This is where a good lawyer will interrupt and suggest that you continue that part of the conversation in private. Not all lawyers will do so. For one thing, he or she might not realize that you want to keep that portion of the conversation under wraps. After all, you're the one blabbering about it. Play it safe. Discuss privileged information before the third party enters the meeting, after he, she, or they leave the meeting, or in a separate meeting altogether.

The lawyer/client privilege borders on being a sacred right in this country. It can be violated only if you allow it to happen.

Lawyers often take a bum rap in this country and sometimes justifiably so. But John Locke wrote, "Wherever law ends, tyranny begins." Without law and lawyers we developers would be subject to the tyranny of chaos. We'd be victims of every whim of an angry or greedy government bureaucrat, neighborhood protective group, supplier, customer, or whacko of any number of stripes out there. Lawyers are essential members of your team. It's one of the most important personnel decisions you'll ever make.

Mark Pearlstein's Secrets

1. For conversion buildings, don't skimp on the exterior wall renovation. Spend more than you anticipate.
2. When the first board is elected, focus on their units and make sure you address *their* punch list items.
3. Concentrate your renovation work on the most common sources of water infiltration: the roof, windows, and exterior walls.
4. Be careful what you promise. Glossy sales brochures promising luxurious lobbies and other building amenities will bind you to complete them.
5. Leave associations with no money and they will sue.
6. Communicate with the owners while controlling the association board. Owners will sue only developers they don't like.
7. Face the owners at a meeting. It is cheaper to take some heat, or verbal abuse, than to defend a lawsuit.
8. Appoint owners to be minority members of the developer board. Involving purchasers in the operation of the association at the earliest possible time will minimize difficulties after turnover.
9. Don't manage your own development, certainly not for the long term. You may be a great property manager, but you are still the developer and, therefore, tainted. New boards want to choose their own manager.
10. Control your sales agents. Give them a script and make sure they stick to it. Loose sales talk will hurt you later.
11. Remember the building entrance sets the tone for the development and sets off the unit owners. Finish the lobby, and make sure the landscaping you install survives the first year.

Mark D. Pearlstein is an attorney at law in Chicago specializing in representing condominium associations and real estate developers. He is a columnist with *The Chicago Tribune.*

CHAPTER 4

Financial

The great secret of success in life is for a man to be ready when his opportunity comes.

Benjamin Disraeli

What is interesting about the Disraeli quote above is it spells out the real business that you are thinking about or now involved in. The real estate development business is the business of opportunity. When I am asked what I look for in real estate, I always answer, "Opportunity!"

Being ready in real estate development often refers to "ready cash." You need access to capital not only to get your project rolling, but to keep it rolling and probably to maintain that roll longer than your original plan envisions. Certainly I recommend a long-haul approach to business success. I also recommend taking a year or more before committing to your first project. Take more than that if you require. I read in the April 11, 2004, *Chicago Tribune* real estate section about a developer who is beginning a development after ten years of planning. Her story is rather complex, but she is a person who realizes that taking time places time on your side. Ten is a lot of years, but when you're ready to move you want to be in a position to, well, get moving. You don't want to start scrambling for money or anything else at the point of entry.

Access to good financing and sound financial advice means cultivating relationships with your area's financial institutions and the appropriate people within them. It's putting on your best suit and your best face. It's meeting and greeting, making presentations and good impressions, and it's continual follow up with your contacts. It's all about the money, but you can't get to the money without getting to know the people. Those people will need to have the same attributes you seek in a lawyer (or financial advisor, contractor, etc.):

- Knowledge
- A good local reputation
- Solid real estate experience

A wise and experienced financial advisor is an essential member of your team. The advisor may be a single person, several individuals, a team within a financial institution, or all of the above. Chances are your advisor(s) will change over time. That's the nature of modern banking. Changes in the economy, mergers, and acquisitions mean that banks and banking personnel are more fluid than ever in our history. Yes, it's a good idea to build strong bonds with specific individuals in the financial industry (banks, savings associations, and so on), but as I noted earlier, changes in management or ownership happen all the time. The connection you've invested years in developing could be fired, transferred, or promoted overnight. Where are you then?

Develop Lots of Financial Relationships

I work very hard at researching financial institutions, and I work even harder at researching qualified individuals within those institutions. This is a constant but necessary task. Change is the nature of modern banking, and real estate developers must adapt to those changes. This is the industry from which we draw the lifeblood of our business—money. Without it, everything dries up and blows away.

It's good to have a banker (savings association officer, etc.) you trust and with whom you feel comfortable doing business.

Even if your contact individual isn't fired, transferred, or promoted, things at the institution can change. Loan policies change. Loan committee personnel changes. Management changes. Lending limits change. Many of the events that can have a significant impact on your business are simply out of your control. Build as many options into your business operation as you can.

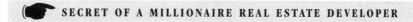

SECRET OF A MILLIONAIRE REAL ESTATE DEVELOPER

15. Build relationships with several financial institutions.

While writing this book, I acted as a Realtor, brokering a 63-unit apartment complex in the Chicago suburb of Aurora. The buyers were a husband and wife I knew through other transactions. Unfortunately, the community bank that they had used for other deals was under a cease and desist order from the FDIC. They were not aware of this and wasted a lot of time trying to get financing for the purchase from this bank. Because it never happened, I had to work overtime helping them obtain financing elsewhere.

I know of businesspeople who have never missed a payment on a loan who have had their loans called because they "no longer fit the profile" of a good risk. Get that. The bank has a good customer who is making his or her payments, someone who's never missed a note or even come in late with a payment. Yet, the new owners or new managers impose a computer-generated template of what a good customer should look like. To heck with history, they say, we've got the template. They might as well be saying, "To heck with our good customers."

As TV-western gambler Bret Maverick might say, "You always need an ace in the hole." Your ace is another banker or two in readiness. Those hold cards will take a lot of the gambling out of your real estate enterprises. I always have to add new lenders to my list because of mergers, acquisitions, and changing loan requirements.

Understand Banking as a Business

Even with the strongest of personal relationships in a financial institution, you must realize that the bank is in business to conduct business. They're not a charity or an organization set up to "do good" in the community. Certainly, most banks are involved in their communities, and just the fact that they do what they do is a terrific benefit to the individuals, families, businesses, and organizations living there. But banking is still a business. The employees in those imposing buildings might even be your friends, but never forget that they're not in business to be your friend. Their purpose, just like yours, is to turn a profit. If you can help each other, "Well, come on in!"

Invest a little time to learn how banks and savings associations work. I don't mean take a course in banking or anything of that depth. Just familiarize yourself with the workings, the committees, and the personnel involved. It's important that you "talk the talk" when dealing with the financial world. There's a bit of that talk presented at the end of this chapter, but you'll need to do some additional homework on your own.

Be prepared for every financial meeting as if it were the most important of your life. As a general rule, that happens many times during your real estate career. Make sure any documentation you need is complete, in order, and in presentation form. Think the meeting through well before you attend. Anticipate the questions you'll get, formulate your answers, and even practice your presentation. Remember, money is the lifeblood of your business, and it's OPM—other people's money—you're using. See that you treat the lifeblood and its caretakers with the respect they're due.

Listen to the Experts

Of course, to listen to the experts you first have to find them and then ask the right questions. I'm approached all the time by people seeking advice and counsel on real estate matters, and unless there's some extenuating circumstance, I'm more than willing to help out. You'll find most people in real estate are that way. Helping others is good for the old ego, but it's also healthy for the industry to help create good developers. Providing sound advice, especially to people just starting out, is an excellent means of building your network of friends, associates, and allies, too.

Make the effort to find a mentor, someone who really knows the ins and outs of this business and who will be willing to take you on as a "project." That's not as intimidating as it may sound. The business is full of people who are flattered at being asked for such guidance. Obviously, you'll want to find experts in buying, selling, and managing real estate properties. You'll also want to find and cultivate experts in banking and the other important areas of real estate development.

Look around your community for the top people in the industry and the allied industries. Who's the best banker in town? Who's the most knowledgeable? Who's the most accessible? How sound is the institution? Is the "old expert" up to date on the latest banking trends relating to real estate? Make a list of several good names because you may have to ask several people. These are busy folks, and you're timing may not match their schedule. Someone in the midst of a huge and complex project just may not have the time to mentor someone. The heart may be willing, but the schedule just might not permit. Other people may already be mentoring someone and will not want to divide their valuable time. Rest easy. You'll find someone.

As I said, the industry is full of extremely generous people who are sincere in their desire to see the business grow, prosper, and become more and more professional.

Here's a key bit of advice. Bankers, and other suppliers, are and should be interested in building their own careers and businesses. That is as it should be. You want to find the individuals and companies who realize the best way to build business is through dedicated service to their customers.

Also, never waste an opportunity. If you're in the presence of a knowledgeable real estate developer, lawyer, banker, or other professional and if you don't believe you'll be interrupting an important conversation, introduce yourself. Say you admire his or her work and you'd appreciate an opinion on a certain matter. I think you'll be surprised at just how many top people are willing to lend a hand to someone coming up the ladder.

Here's a strong word of advice when seeking the opinions of others. Find people who are happy in their work. I don't care how successful a person may appear in the business, if he or she isn't happy doing that work, you don't want their opinions. I've seen people just starting out in this most wonderful of businesses almost crushed because they've sought advice from some sour old case of burnout. Earlier I made mention that the meanest and toughest SOBs are often very high-profile people, but they're not necessarily the most successful in the long term. They're certainly not the happiest or the most inspirational people either. Look for the men and women who are excited about their work and who just can't wait for the next business day to begin. Those are the people you want to emulate. Those are your mentors.

Start with Your Community Bank

I recommend lots of banking relationships with lots of financial institutions, but because I'm still very big on community banking, that's where I recommend you begin building those relationships. It's easy for real estate novices to grab the financial section of the newspaper or make a few phone calls for best "deal" on interest rates, closing costs, and other real estate and financial matters. That's all valuable information, but there's more to being a millionaire real estate developer than crunching numbers.

A small, community bank is usually staffed with people who are more able to invest one-on-one time with their customers. That's only natural. Like those old ads for the second-place auto rental company, they're smaller so they have to "try harder" to earn your business. That's a real plus for you. Often the value of that personal service far outweighs the sometimes broader and perhaps more sophisticated services offered by larger, regional banks. Naturally, you'll still want to conduct a good bit of in-depth research before aligning yourself with any bank, even a friendly and aggressive one.

When I call my bank, I like to know that someone I'm familiar with will be on the other end of the line, not just the next person in rotation. There's often an important advantage for real estate developers in working with community banks. They tend to be more interested in the community. That's just natural. The managers and committees aren't concerned about or affected by what's happening in the branch locations three counties or three states away. This local focus can give you a real leg up in getting the financing and financial advice you need.

Among the services you'll need from any bank are these seven:

1. Mortgage for your own home
2. Construction loans and mortgages for real estate development properties
3. Refinancing for home and/or real estate properties
4. A line of credit for real estate purchases
5. Long-term mortgages
6. Escrow accounts for funds held on behalf of someone purchasing one of your properties
7. Personal banking services (checking, savings, consumer loans, and so on)

All banks and savings associations can provide these and other services, but I still like to know that people recognize me when I call or walk in the door. I may be a big fish in a little pond, but the services of my community bank keep my business swimming along nicely. That works well for the novices in this business, too. The way to become a big fish is to start small, and a small, community bank usually makes for a terrific place to get your feet wet.

A Few Important Terms

If you haven't already begun your financial education, please begin immediately. If you don't understand the lifeblood of the industry, you'll do a lot of unnecessary bleeding. Remember the big "con" of this industry: you may lose a lot of money. If you develop a sound understanding of finance and financial principals, you'll also be able to enjoy the big "pro" of our industry: you can make a lot of money.

Let's begin your education with the definition of a few important terms. Again, this little introduction is just to get you started. You'll have to do most of the swimming in these uncharted waters on your own. That's the best way to learn—sink or swim.

- *Finance:* In real estate development, the word refers to borrowing money to buy and develop property. Whether your interest is in raw land, industrial property, commercial real estate, residential developments, apartments, shopping centers, retail outlets, highrise buildings or whatever, very few of us have the ability to make such purchases out of our own pockets. We need OPM—other people's money.
- *Finance charge:* Interest and perhaps other fees or charges attached to the loan of money. It's like buying anything else on credit, except that you're dealing on a significantly greater scale.
- *Financial leverage:* This is an important term that refers to using borrowed money to buy property. As a general rule, it is far better to use financial leverage than your own money for real estate development.
- *Financial statement:* An accounting of, well, your account, showing your income, expenses, assets, liabilities, and equity. It's a financial snapshot of your condition at a given point in time.
- *Creative financing:* Basically, that's coming up with the money you need by any means other than the traditional route of a mortgage loan. Options include balloon payment loans, wraparound mortgages, assumption mortgages, sale-leasebacks, land contracts, and other methods. I've discovered that the adage holds especially true for a millionaire real estate developer: "Where there's a will, there's a way."
- *Line of credit:* This term describes a very handy arrangement to have with your financial institutions. It's a financial instrument that lets you borrow up to a limited amount of money without having to jump through the hoops of applying for an additional loan. You're still borrowing money and you still have to pay it back, but you just can't

overestimate the value of having ready cash in real estate development. Lines of credit will be among your most valuable tools.

 **SECRET OF A MILLIONAIRE REAL ESTATE DEVELOPER**

16. Think like a millionaire real estate developer.

If you adopt the mindset of a millionaire real estate developer, you'll find yourself adopting the habits that come with the territory. At that point, you really can't help but become a member of the club. Your goal is "mind accomplished," and that's half the battle right there because then you're ready to take on the physical steps that will take you to that goal. One of the most powerful means of getting ready for those steps involves the acquisition of financing and financial advisors. I advise that you start taking those first steps right now.

Here's a case in point. Many of my most successful real estate deals could only have been accomplished with lines of credit established with community banks. One episode in particular involved the purchase of a 24-unit rental building in a post-foreclosure sale from the lender who had title to the property. In 1999, I was chasing a mixed-use rental property in a popular neighborhood in Chicago known as Ravenswood. I bought that property but also learned that the lender involved had foreclosed on a 24-unit rental property in a less desirable area of Chicago known as Woodlawn.

I was encouraged to look at the property, and I called a community banker to look at the property with me. I knew this man for many years, and his community bank was located near this property. I knew that he knew the area well, and I knew that he would lend on the property if I wanted to purchase it. I had lines of credit ready, and when my new banker/old friend told me how great this find was, I used the lines of credit to "pay cash" to close the acquisition fast. I then refinanced with the community bank, placing a mortgage on the property and paying off the credit lines. That allowed me to use the credit lines for other opportunities. Thus I really bought the property with none of my own money down—a perfect situation. Even though I used a significant part of the cash flow to improve the property, I made nothing but money during the five years I owned the property. I sold it in January of 2004 for just under a $1-million profit. Not bad for a no-money-down deal. If it were not for the credit lines, I could never have had that opportunity.

Jay Fahn's Top Ten Ways to Help Your Own Case When Applying for a Commercial Real Estate Loan

1. Submit a formal and *current* personal financial statement. Be sure to sign and date it.
2. Show gross assets (current market value) and gross liabilities (mortgage balance) when listing investments in real estate. Showing "net equity" is not useful and wastes time in the underwriting process.
3. Attach copies of asset accounts (i.e., banks, securities) for most recent months. (This is a *big* plus.)
4. Have copies of your two most recent tax returns including any K-1s.
5. If refinancing, include Schedule E or the appropriate K-1.
6. Make any expense deposit quickly and without quibbling. (Amateurs argue over expense deposits.)
7. Explain the ownership structure early and in detail. Have all LLC and partnership organizational documents available.
8. Order the survey in a timely manner.
9. Don't save negative information for the last minute.
10. Call the bank on a regular basis and ask if my additional information is required.

Jay Fahn is the Vice President of the Hyde Park Bank in Chicago.

CHAPTER 5

Accounting

Two and two continue to make four, in spite of the whine of the amateur for three, or the cry of the critic for five.

James Abbott McNeill Whistler

Dictionaries define *accounting* as a "system, science, or art" of maintaining, analyzing, and explaining commercial accounts. The word has entered popular culture as a means of settling accounts or in some cases settling up old scores. When someone says, "There's going to be an accounting," you know exactly what the speaker means. It's keeping the books, crunching the numbers, or any number of clever phrases, but most important, it's a means of knowing financially where you've been, where you are, and where you're most likely headed. Look at it this way. If money is the lifeblood of real estate, then accounting is your heart monitor.

Accounting versus Bookkeeping

In the old days, the bookkeeper was the nice lady down the street who kept the books for families and small businesses who had very simple and basic financial needs. She noted down income and outgo, drew a line, and said "This is what's left." Her pay was $100 a week or so.

That's fine, but it's not accounting, and it's certainly no way to keep track of your financial blood pressure. A millionaire real estate developer has a special place on the team for a talented accountant or accounting firm. He or she or the firm is one of the knights of your round table, equal in stature and responsibility to your other key players. Real estate development, even at its most basic and simplest stages, represents a considerable amount of financial business. You're wheeling and dealing with a lot of suppliers engaged in complex tasks in a variety of industries: architects, interior designers, planners, construction personnel, plumbers, electricians, lawyers, government bureaucrats, and on and on. You've got to know where you are at all times. That's especially true of your financial condition. Without that knowledge base upon which to act you'll soon find your business in "serious condition" as that term is used down at the ER. Again, your expert must have up-to-date knowledge of the industry, a good local reputation, and a solid background in real estate.

The services of a top accountant or accounting firm are key to your success. As with the other key players, don't waste time looking.

SECRET OF A MILLIONAIRE REAL ESTATE DEVELOPER

17. Hire a great accountant.

What Does an Accountant Do?

As I've just indicated, an accountant handles far more and far more significant chores than just keeping the books. You should expect your accountant to work with you all the time and not just sit in the office waiting for orders. He or she should invest some time just "thinking ahead" about your business and its probable needs. He should anticipate how changes in law, regulation, government personnel, the economy, and other factors will impact your business. She should be looking to next year, the year after, and the year after that. This is a business partnership with you sitting at the head of the table, but part of what you're buying is this individual's ability to gaze into a crystal ball.

Services will vary somewhat from client to client, but generally speaking an accountant should provide the following:

- Sound financial advice and counsel
- Record keeping
- Financial record analysis
- Business (financial) analysis
- Tax preparation and filing
- Preparation or input of financial portions of business proposals
- Assistance with loan presentation
- Evaluation of business insurance coverage
- Personal insurance needs evaluation
- Advice on investments, including areas other than real estate
- Advice on obtaining and maintaining (or regaining) creditworthiness
- Estate planning
- Retirement planning
- Regular reporting, at least once a quarter
- Input on corporate salary structures, bonuses, benefits, retirement plans, etc.

Working with a Great Accountant

As you might suspect, working with an accountant is a partnership in which each party has certain responsibilities. I've just mentioned some of the key duties, but two overriding qualities I think are essential in any accountant or accounting firm.

These are objectivity coupled with courage. Too many accountants knuckle under when pressure is applied by a client. They tell the boss what he or she wants to hear rather than what the boss should hear and needs to hear. If you followed the early twenty-first century scandals on Wall Street, you probably noticed that prominent accounting firms were right in the middle of that mess. These firms allowed their client's problems to become their own. They'd have been far better off in the long run had they summoned up the courage to be objective with their clients and do the right thing.

That's what a millionaire real estate developer wants and needs—objectivity. You can't fix a problem if you don't know the problem exists. If, for whatever reason, your accountant is too timid or too intimidated to tell you of such problems, you may not have the time or the opportunity to fix them when the crisis boils over. As you prepare any project, you'll want to go over the details and you should expect an objective opinion of the good and bad factors involved. You don't want someone agreeing with your every statement simply because you're name appears on their monthly check. You want and need someone willing to ask challenging questions and to make you think about what you're about to do. "That's well and good, Mr. Client, but have you considered . . ."

You're the boss and everything in business is management directed. How are you really directing your suppliers? Are you asking them to look the other way or are you demanding their honest and best efforts? Many a good manager has slipped up and allowed himself or herself to buy into numbers that have been "massaged" to make the boss feel better, more secure, or more important. In the long run that's a sure road to disaster. Constant self monitoring is in order.

Again, a relationship is a two-way street. As a millionaire real estate developer you have to carry your share of the responsibilities, and those responsibilities extend beyond signing that monthly check. It's essential that you bring honesty to the table. If you "doctor" the numbers to present a false picture, provide inadequate documentation, or if you're just sloppy, you could cause a lot of self-inflicted financial grief. If you've done your homework, conducted your interviews properly, and have made a sound decision, your selection is worthy of your trust. Give it.

Again, your chores will vary according to the dictates of your business, but here are a few guidelines. Let's assume that you're meeting with your new accountant for the first time. What should you bring? At that first meeting have

- income tax records for the past two to five years;
- earnings, a list as itemized as possible of how much money you're making from all sources;
- how much you've paid in local, state, and federal taxes and the dates of filing;
- date of purchase, purchase price, date of sale, and profits from the sale of any securities within the past year;

- any items you can legally deduct from your income tax (business expenses, medical costs, donations to recognized charities, loan interest, etc.);
- any improvements and the costs of those improvements to properties you own;
- closing or escrow papers on any property you've purchased;
- closing papers from the original purchase if you have sold any property;
- any items about which you have a financial question; and
- anything your accountant asks you to bring. Yes, ask if there's anything you should bring to the meeting before you show up at the meeting.

Four Essential Reports

Your accountant will provide a number of reports. You may require additional or specialized reporting, too. I've found that just about everyone in this business needs four very specific and very important financial documents. Numbers *can* lie. They can be manipulated and shoved around to appear to produce any number of false or inadequate conclusions. To be successful in the long run, you need accountants who have the courage to present honest numbers objectively. These documents, properly prepared, will provide you with a wealth of information, information you'll use ideally to build wealth. Here's a brief description. Be sure to discuss the following four documents with your accountant or accountant candidate:

1. *Balance sheet:* Lists your assets and your liabilities at a specific point in time. "This is what you have/don't have today." In most cases, your accountant provides a balance sheet at the end of the accounting period. Of course, you can get one at any time, and in many cases you certainly don't want to wait for the end of any accounting period to get an accurate look at your financial status.
2. *Income statement:* An itemized accounting of all your revenues versus operating expenses for a given period of time, say a financial quarter or a year. Because this document states your profits and/or losses, it is sometimes referred to as a profit-and-loss statement.
3. *Cash flow analysis:* The lifeblood of your business is always flowing. This document tells you whether the money is flowing as income or

as outgo. If we're thinking in those terms, I think you'll agree that it's far better to have that lifeblood inside a healthy body.

4. *Quick asset ratio:* Compares your liquid assets, those that can be sold in a year or less and called current assets, against your current liabilities, also known as short-term liabilities, that can be sold off or eliminated in a year or less.

Description of a Great Accountant

It should go without saying that your accountant should know accounting as it relates to real estate and particularly to real estate development. Apparently it's not said enough because I know many very good real estate people who are not being well-served by their accountants who, by the way, are also very good. It's not that the accountants are lazy, indifferent, or without skills. They work very hard from what I can tell. The problem is that they're not real estate accountants. Real estate is a very specialized field, and their real estate clients suffer due to their lack of knowledge and experience. A great accountant for you is one who knows real estate, preferably someone with a good bit of experience.

I used an accountant before I began in the real estate development field. He was great for the nuts and bolts of everyday accounting, but from 1986 on real estate accounting changed dramatically. The Tax Reform Act of 1986 disallowed benefits that are now only blessed memory. The years from 1986 through 1991 were phase-in years, and since that time the tax laws for real estate have always been changing. Much of what my accountant learned at the time was due to my own independent research. I taught him real estate accounting and paid him to learn too. I did not have the heart to change accountants due to the loyalty this older man had shown me over the years. But if I knew then what I knew now, I would have simply explained that my business had changed and would have made the change before his retirement.

I noted that your attorney should have some basic understanding of accounting. Well, vice versa is true. It is essential that your accounting and legal teams work "on the same page" and as a team. A great accountant will have a basic understanding of real estate law and will be able to converse intelligently with your lawyer without the need of a United Nation's interpreter. I actually use an attorney who is also a CPA for my legal and accounting needs.

You should look for expertise in your line of work. Remember, when using two professionals, you will be paying folks who will probably be working on hourly rates. All that time spent discussing and explaining jargon and terminology is on your nickel.

A great accountant will have a great reputation. Again, ask around. Get references. Call the professional associations and business groups. The chamber of commerce isn't going to recommend one member over another, but knowing who is a member will show you who is active in the business community and that's a good sign. A report from the Better Business Bureau can indicate certain individuals and firms to avoid. Simply asking your friends and associates in business can help you develop a list of "possibles" and automatic "rejects."

You should ask for and expect to receive promptly a list of references. Some of these references should be from successful real estate developers. Too many people get such a list and think, "Well, he must be okay," and then move on. Please! Check the references. Make the calls. Ask the questions. This person or these people will have their hands on the lifeblood of your business. Make doubly sure they know what they're doing.

A great accountant will be able and willing to provide a detailed list of fees and charges and how those items are structured. Does he or she charge for phone calls? Probably not, but it's a good idea to find out. What's the hourly rate? What are the rates of other people in the office and what tasks will they be assigned on your account? It's okay to ask for a "guesstimate" to get an idea of how much charges might run on a given project. You don't want to try to tie someone down to a figure before he or she can crunch the numbers—and say so. You just want an idea of the overall fees. A price range of a high and a low is okay. Again, in the initial stage you just want an idea of what you might be getting into.

Tell your accountant that you expect him or her to stay up to speed on changes in law and regulation affecting the accounting portion of your business and to keep you informed. As a millionaire real estate developer you just won't have time to stay on top of such changes. That's part of what you're paying all these top professionals to do.

Ask for a client list. This will give you a good idea of the quality of work provided by your prospective accounting firm. As a general rule, top-notch companies hire top-notch suppliers. There are, of course, exceptions to the rule. That's why you make all those calls to the references.

You or your business may have additional requirements. The dictates of your market, such as a need for bilingual communication, may impose others.

But to me the above requirements are the essentials. Most essential of all is, obviously, a knowledge of and familiarity with accounting for real estate development.

Big Fish or Little Fish?

There's always a quandary when hiring suppliers. Is it better to hire a large firm with a large staff and resources or is it a wiser move to hire a smaller, leaner company or even an individual? Large companies have a lot of resources, but there's the risk of being just another of many customers, perhaps even being the low person on the totem pole when it comes to service. A smaller company may lack many resources and the staffing of a large company, but they may offer more dedicated one-on-one service. Is it better to be a big fish in a little pond or a little fish in a big pond?

Only you, your business needs, and the abilities of your local suppliers can answer that question. There's no across-the-board right answer, and whatever answer you arrive at may change over time. The best advice I can give has already been given. Do your homework. Once you've evaluated the truly important aspects of each candidate, go with your gut feeling. Hire the person or the firm you honestly believe will give you the very best service for your specific needs. Whoever fills that niche, regardless of size, is your accountant. As Goldilocks would say, they're "just right."

What About Accounting Software?

Personally, I am "underwhelmed." From my research so far, the so-called accounting software programs out there really aren't accounting programs. They're bookkeeping programs, and, as far as that goes, some of them are just fine. But they can't really handle the specialized needs for real estate development accounting. Someone or some company may come out with the perfect software tomorrow, but as of today I have not seen it.

It's not that they can't handle the math. They can't handle the regulation. Real estate is a heavily regulated industry. Local, county, state, and federal bureaucrats are always making changes in real estate law and regulation. Software developers just can't keep up with the pace of change. Who could?

A simple change in a single code could make an expensive, sophisticated software package obsolete overnight. Worse, not taking that change into account could cost you a fortune and possibly do great damage to a project or even your company. Look, you know someone in the federal government is going to make some change within any given year. Any software program you buy is automatically dated by the time you buy your next calendar. Toss in the efforts of your state government, your county, and your local municipal guardians of democracy and it's no wonder software programmers can't keep up.

This is why we hire accountants. They can keep up and they can adjust. They'd better keep up and they'd better adjust or we'll just flip through the old yellow pages and find someone who will. And the good accountants know that.

That being said, I'm perfectly comfortable recommending the use of software programs solely for bookkeeping purposes. There are many packages out there, and a lot of them are very useful and quite handy to have at the end of the year when you need accurate records and documentation. Visit with your accountant before you buy a program and get his or her recommendation. You'll want your systems to be compatible and, being an expert, he or she should be able to guide you towards the best, most flexible, and most economical purchase.

Two and two still make four—always have, always will. We get into trouble when our ego, our greed, our fear, or some other emotion motivates us to attempt to make two and two come out to another number. It just won't work. That's why we have accountants, professionals who know their jobs, understand our business, and who have the courage and objectivity to state the obvious. Those are the type of people you want on your accounting team. Those are the folks who'll help you become a millionaire real estate developer. Count on it.

CHAPTER 6

Construction, Maintenance, and Repair

Every great man exhibits the talent of organization or construction, whether it be in a poem, a philosophical system, a policy, or a strategy. And without method there is no organization nor construction.

Edward Bulwer-Lytton

The way someone in this business develops his or her real estate is through construction. That construction, and the profits derived from it through the years, are assured through maintenance and repair. Although there is an obvious overlap of knowledge, skills, and responsibilities, they are really two different areas of responsibility. *Construction* is an act of creation, or in some cases recreation when you refurbish or remodel an existing structure. Either way, you're building something, changing something, adding on, or taking away something. *Maintenance* and *repair* are more concerned with keeping what has been constructed in good working order and getting things back to normal when order breaks down.

A large part of my typical working day involves working with contractors in construction, maintenance, and repair. As a developer I'm actively involved in all three areas. You'll find yourself in the same position once you start your journey to millionaire real estate developer status. I've worked with some of the best and the worst in the business. Over the years I've developed three guidelines for working with the industry. I think you'll find them help-ful in your real estate ventures.

1. Plan on the worst. Yes, I believe in hoping for the best, but I base my business plans on my vision of the worst possible scenario. Things happen, and it's best to have a plan ready to be put in place than to be scrambling around trying to pick up the pieces of a catastrophe at the last moment.

2. Never begin any project without a written contract that includes all important specifications. You should also build in a fixed deadline for completion or even a series of deadlines throughout the construc-tion period. I have a policy of never allowing a contractor or a sub-contractor on any of my properties unless a sound contract is in place and their insurance is certificated. Also, if you write up your own contracts, avoid "legalese." That's legal language or too often gob-bledygook that sounds like it ought to be legal language. Without a background in law, you could unintentionally write yourself into a legal bind. Leave the fancy words to the lawyers, and write your doc-uments in plain, easy-to-understand English.

3. If your contractors require a deposit, negotiate the smallest figure possible. I believe in a pay-as-you-go policy. Pay in progress billings or on the progress of the job. Set realistic deadlines and pay as the con-tractor meets them. Make sure your contractors sign a "waiver of lien" before you make any payments, including the down payment. This document protects you from the contractor declaring nonpay-ment, which could put your project in jeopardy while the tedious legal maneuverings take place. Even if you win all the legal battles, your construction could fall seriously behind schedule. Falling be-hind schedule could and often does lead to dire consequences, fi-nancial difficulties, and perhaps even more legal action.

Once you've covered these three bases, you should be in pretty good shape for proceeding with your construction. That's not to say you won't ex-perience any hassles. Anything is possible. I've worked with a lot of contrac-tors, and, with a few exceptions, they've always performed well. I just believe that by taking care of these three items up front, I'm helping them perform even better.

Always Get Construction Permits

Sometimes jumping through all the legal hoops you face seems like a real hassle. Sometimes it is, but it's also necessary, proper, and in your best interests. There's always a temptation for some to skirt the law, but it's been my experience that those who do don't get away with the practice for long and that the eventual price tag just isn't worth the effort.

Suppose you beat the system during construction. What exactly have you earned? A likely answer is something called a "stop work order" from the supervising municipality. This little document will have a major negative impact on your deadline and your profit margin. Not only will you have to undo all the improper construction you've completed, but you'll have to start over and invest more time, effort, and money in doing what you should have done in the first place.

SECRET OF A MILLIONAIRE REAL ESTATE DEVELOPER

18. Do things the way things are supposed to be done.

Adopt that rule from day one of your real estate career and all the following days will be much easier.

There's another important consideration. Those rules and regulations, the "hoops" you have to jump through, are in place for very good reasons. How you construct a building, the quality of materials used, and the experience and knowledge of the builders has a direct effect on the soundness and safety of your project. Those hoops are there to protect the health and safety of all who come in, on, under, or around your property. Don't you agree that it's a good idea to use electrical wiring that won't overheat and cause a fire? Isn't it a good idea to build with concrete that won't start crumbling in a few years? What's wrong with allowing handicapped persons access to your property?

Getting the proper permits is generally the responsibility of your contractor. Of course, because overall responsibility for the entire project is in your hands, it's definitely your responsibility to make sure the contractor complies. Follow up. Know what permits will be needed for your project and insist on seeing them. This is one reason it's so important to do that homework I keep harping on. Ask around. Get references and get any warnings out there, too. Follow up on the references and interview potential contractors before you hire them. Every shortcut you take during the selection process can come back and bite you financially during or even after construction.

A good contractor will stay on top of the technology curve. Construction materials, techniques, and equipment are improving all the time. Innovations are being introduced constantly, and many of these new ideas can be of tremendous benefit to the real estate developer provided he or she is in a position to take advantage of them. Only someone in construction who is willing to invest the time to keep up can match the pace of improvements. As with your legal and financial advisors, you want people who know the business, have a good local reputation, and who are up to speed on real estate development law, rules, and regulations. That's the person or the company you want on your team.

We've all heard stories of the outrageous behavior of pinheaded bureaucrats in local government, and some of those stories are true. Still, in the vast majority of dealings I've had with the bureaucrats, I've had very few problems. Most of these people are hardworking individuals who really want to do a good job. As I've said, there are very sound reasons for all those hoops you jump through, and these people are right in insisting that you make the leap. Treat them with the respect they're due and you'll be surprised at the level of cooperation you'll earn.

Always Get Multiple Bids

When I buy a new car I always check with several dealerships. If I feel like cooking up a batch of three-alarm chili, I'll even shop the grocery ads for the best price on beef, onions, and my secret ingredient. Whenever I print a new brochure for my company, I always get multiple printing bids, and I'm always amazed at how varied the estimates can be for a single set of specifications. Sometimes one bid will be as high as 100 percent over another. Same ink, same paper, same number of pages, same amount of type, same processes, and the bids come back with numbers all over the place. You'll find it's the same with contractors.

One of the chief reasons for multiple bids is self-protection. Suppose, despite your homework, you've hooked up with an unscrupulous contractor who overcharges for everything. Without getting other bids, you can never ask the obvious question, "Why is your bid twice that of your competitors?" I have a number of contractors with whom I've worked very satisfactorily for years. They've always done an excellent job, and I plan on working with them for many more years. I still get multiple bids on every job, especially if the low bid is significantly below the other bids. That's usually a good indication that you'll be buying inferior workmanship and/or materials. The later maintenance and repair, and perhaps legal problems, resulting from shoddy work is far more costly than any "savings" you'd make on a ridiculously low bid. Low bidders may run out of money during your project. Delays sap your energy, your production schedule, and your profit margins. You might even have to get a lien release from the contractor so you can get another company to complete the work. So much for those "savings," eh?

 SECRET OF A MILLIONAIRE REAL ESTATE DEVELOPER

19. Work only with licensed, bonded, and insured contractors.

Contractors who are licensed, bonded, and insured have jumped through their own set of hoops. They've proven themselves worthy of an established and accepted set of standards. I just won't work with a contractor who doesn't meet these basic qualifications. Period.

You want to work with the best people. The phrase "Lic., Bnd., & Ins." on a business card is not an absolute guarantee, but it's a good indication of a person or company worthy of further scrutiny. Unethical contractors can cause the developer a world of hurt. For example, sometimes a contractor accepts your money but refuses to pay his subcontractors. Even though it's not technically your fault, it's your project and your responsibility. The unpaid subcontractors can come back and put a lien on your property. It's possible that you could face foreclosure to see that those bills are paid. Again, you've got to be vigilant on every aspect of your development every step of the way.

Four Key Elements of Every Contract

I don't want to get into a lecture on legal matters, and certainly the details put down on paper and in ink will vary from project to project. And you should always consult with your own legal counsel before signing any agreement. (Chapter 11 has some more information on this matter.) Still, I believe the following four elements should be in every construction contract:

1. The developer's right to terminate the relationship with the contractor provided his subcontractors do not meet the specifications or deadlines of the project
2. The developer's right to remove a lien placed on your property
3. A firm completion date and, if necessary, project-specific deadlines within that time frame
4. The developer's protection from the use of substandard materials or workmanship by the contractor or subcontractors

Be Aware of These Three Dirty Tricks

If you've done your homework properly, as all millionaire real estate developers do, you probably won't be working with any unscrupulous contractors. Still, sometimes doing homework doesn't guarantee you'll pass the test. Some contractors are pretty good at fooling developers, at least for a while. Others are good people who come across bad times and adopt bad habits to get them through. And every once in a while a reputable contractor will just "go bad" and cross the line for any number of reasons. There are three common tricks these types of operators may try on you. So, forewarned is forearmed.

Dirty trick number one turns your financing into their bank. What happens is as simple as it is wrong. The contractor needs funds to complete someone else's project. He takes the money you paid as a down payment on your project to complete the other. That problem solved, he then has to find another developer and another down payment so that he can start your work. It's the old scheme of robbing Peter to pay Paul. I had this happen to me with my first renovation and have seen it happen time and time again. The contractor always ends up in bankruptcy court, the job is incomplete, and you have to incur the expense of starting over.

As a real estate developer you have to take responsibility for your money even when it's in the hands of other people or companies. You've hired these people to do a specific job. See that your down payment is applied to that job or you may never see the job completed to your satisfaction.

Dirty trick number two is the use of ghost wages to boost a contractor's profits. In this little scheme the contractor has you paying wages for workers who are like ghosts. They're invisible because they just aren't there. Your contractor will be hiring plumbers, painters, electricians, roofers, and a lot of other people plus their helpers and "grunt" laborers. The opportunity for putting ghost workers on the payroll is ever present and often hard to prove. For example, a plumber (or whatever) may be "hired" for an extra day to handle an unexpected "problem" on the job site. Also, his helper was there all day, too. And then there's the matter of the extra supplies. You weren't on site that day, and even if you were, you probably didn't take inventory of personnel. And here's this bill for eight hours for two men. What are you to do except pay it?

Another way to create ghost wages is simply to charge for more hours than actual hours worked. Some of this you'll have to chalk up to "the cost of doing business." You really can't catch a supplier who occasionally bills three hours for two hours work and in the overall scheme of things, the losses or negligible. It's those who really take advantage of the opportunity that you have to catch. That's where you can really lose big money.

The only answer is eternal vigilance. As a millionaire real estate developer you have to take responsibility for being on site and on guard. That's one of the ways you'll be sure to stay a millionaire real estate developer. Things will always fall through the cracks, but make surprise visits to the job site and see what is going on.

Dirty trick number three is a version of the old bait-and-switch game. You see this scam a lot in retail sales. The customer sees an ad for a new television set (or toaster oven, automobile, or whatever) at a fantastically low price. He or she rushes down to take advantage of the bargain only to discover that "Sorry, we just sold the last one." This is a little hard to believe because it's one minute after the store opened and the customer is the first one through the door. They baited with one thing and then switched to another product, always a more expensive or at least a more profitable one.

How does this work in construction? It starts with a snow job. During your interview you're bombarded with a lot of very professional images. You're handed an expensive company brochure with four-color photographs of their many successful and prestigious projects. You meet a dedicated staff of professionals at their impressive offices. Perhaps you're even taken to a job site where you see a lot of hardworking personnel in company uniforms doing their best for the customer. That's the bait.

The switch comes at your job site when a crew from an entirely different contractor shows up. That's because the company you hired sold your contract to another company or another individual who will actually do the work. After all that homework and research, you've got a completely unknown entity building your development. These new people may be just as good or better than the original, but you have no way of knowing that. And chances are the crew and its management will not be nearly as qualified as the company you invested all that time in researching. The brochures, office personnel, management, and the tour of the job site were all meaningless. Bait and switch.

Let your lawyer handle situations like this before they become problems. Make sure the contract he or she writes for you has a clause stating that it is nonassignable. The contractor you hire can't then turn around and sell (assign) your job to a third party.

This isn't the last time you'll read the words "I learned this the hard way" in this book. One of my early challenges as a developer was renovating an owner's unit in a three-unit building, one I still own. It was a 6,000 square foot house on a 50 × 150 foot lot with two two-car garages. It had been converted into a three-family building during the post World War II housing shortage. The owner, Mr. Crab, was a developer who had built many homes in this suburb since the 1950s. If you drive through the Chicago suburb of Wilmette, you will observe Crab Apple Lane, Crab Apple Drive, Crab Apple Cove, Crab Tree Lane, Crab Tree Drive, and other similar names.

The house had been well-maintained but was showing its age. My wife and I wanted to customize the second floor and use that as our home. We wanted to install a fireplace, marble bathroom, a whirlpool tub, Corian counters, a double convection oven, and other modern amenities. We hired a general contractor who had done work for me before. He was a great guy, and we had done a lot of good work together. He always delivered on time and met all my deadlines on schedule. I had always found his prices to be reasonable.

As work progressed, I hired him to do even more on the property, including some changes to the common area. Unfortunately, at the time we were beginning this project, his dad retired, leaving the business to his less than capable son. That became a big, big problem—my problem. Sonny Boy may have been his dad's biological son, but he was an acorn who had fallen far from the tree. While supposedly working on my project, he took on other projects and was taking money from one job to finish other jobs. He had no loyalty to his father's business, reputation, commitments, and certainly not to me.

My wife and I would arrive at the property to find that work was uncompleted. Sometimes he and his crew were even working other jobs when they were supposed to be taking care of my project. He wouldn't return my phone calls. Yelling at him whenever I could track him down did nothing at all. He was an individual lacking any sense of responsibility. Some contractors pull this kind of stunt all the time, and millionaire real estate developers have to know how to deal with the situation.

What finally set me off was a confrontation with his concrete subcontractor. I noticed that the recently-poured patio was cracking. When I called the subcontractor, he became angry and said that he had not been paid by the general contractor, whom I *had* paid. This is another common problem real estate developer's face. I had gotten to know the members of this firm's team of carpenters, and when I called the senior carpenter on the job, he said he and his people hadn't been paid either by the son. This set me off because I had been paying Sonny Boy's bills all along, although I should have noticed that the son had a new SUV and two cell phones.

I asked the carpenter if he would work if I took Sonny Boy out of the loop and paid him directly. "Sure," was the answer. I hired all the skilled workers necessary to complete the job. In essence I became my own general contractor. The lesson to be learned here is to check and to review the partial and final lien-waivers supplied by subcontractors before disbursing any payments. Paying your workers really works. Working successfully with contractors is just that simple. Make sure that your contractor is paying his subcontractors and employees. Because you're the developer, it's your responsibility.

This chapter began with a quote about the importance of organization. Successful developers are very organized people because they know advance planning and appropriate action ahead of time takes care of problematical situations long before they can ever become problems.

Secrets of Working with Contractors, from Perry Peterson

Size of the Contractor

It's important to pick a contractor that is large enough to handle your project. A single contractor can get overwhelmed, which can lead to costly delays and other related problems. On the other hand, if you're a small developer working with a large contractor, your project could get lost in the shuffle or given a low priority. Get several bids on each project. This helps you understand the job and to gather valuable input. Each contractor will have a different view of your job and how it should be done. Each will also have comments on the types of materials to use.

Insurance

Make sure your contractor and architect have insurance. It's for your protection and your neighbor's protection as much as it is for the contractor. Also request automobile insurance that covers any contractors and the personal vehicles of any workers. Shrubs, lawns, fences, garages, and houses have been damaged by contractor vehicles. Your insurance agent can provide you a list of the types of insurance and the limits you should require.

References

Get references from developers who have handled projects similar to yours in size and budget. It is important that you go beyond looking at pictures and a few phone calls. Ask for jobs in progress that you can visit. Stop at previous jobs and ask about workmanship, materials, schedules, and budgets. Replacing a poor contractor due to his failure on any or all of the above items can be very costly. Stop at his or her office to look for licenses, awards, and affiliations. Check with the Better Business Bureau. Once you've done all of the above, you'll have a good sense of who your contractor is and whether you can work with him or her or not. This will also help you better understand the scope of your job.

Determine the Scope of the Work

It is important that you define the materials to be used as well as the size and types of rooms in your project. Decide which rooms are to be carpeted, wood-floored, tiled, etc. It doesn't stop here. There are many types of windows, countertops, appliances, and cabinets. Types of wood trim, paint, wall coverings, and window coverings should also be considered. You may hire an interior designer to bring it all together to save you time and frustration. The better you define the work and the materials, the happier you will be with the outcome. This also will help you better understand the different uses of materials and the processes to install them. If you are using your own architect or your contractor's, it is important you check his or her references in the same manner as the contractors. The architect is one half of your team. Once the work starts, visit the site often in order to keep aware of the progress and allow for timely changes, which generally means less cost.

Permits

Make sure your contract has the contractor or architect responsible for permits. Getting them is not your responsibility, but making sure your contractor does so *is* your responsibility. There's nothing worse than finding out that you've built too close to a lot line or that you can only build to half the size you need. Contractors are the professionals and are in a much better position to meet the permit requirements. Inspections by the governing jurisdiction also help ensure your structure is being properly built. Failure to get permits can also stop the sale of the property at a future date as well as make you potentially liable after the sale if the property does not comply with local zoning or codes.

Schedules

Request a timeline schedule from the contractor that defines the cost of items (commonly called a schedule of values) in the schedule. The schedule of values will break out such things as concrete—foundation, sidewalk, drives, and carpentry—rough, trim, cabinets. This helps you and the contractor agree on the dollar value of the work in place as the job progresses and is also very helpful in setting a schedule you both agree on.

Contract

Read and understand the contract, whether it's yours or the contractor's. It should spell out the contractor's work and responsibilities and not relieve him or her from them. It should address how payouts are made and spell out down payments, if any at all. You, your contractor, and your architect should inspect the work together to agree on the value of payouts. The contract should have a method of issuing a change order so you can add or delete items contracted for. You should attach the schedules you have gotten from the contractor and make them part of the contract. It's advisable to withhold some monies to ensure all work has been properly completed. This money should not be dispersed until after a final walk-through to ensure all punch list items have been completed. The contract should also spell out the items you have defined in your scope of work as well as warrantees. Have an attorney review the contract. If any issues arise, this is the document that decides them.

Waivers

As work progresses and contractors are paid, they should submit partial waivers and then a final waiver upon completion. These are important because they show that contractors and their suppliers have been paid. If the heating contractor installs a furnace, his or her waiver should show the cost of the furnace and the labor cost to install it. A carpenter would have lumberyard and labor costs on his or her waiver. These are important as they help avoid liens at a later date and help establish a dollar value and time schedule.

Punch List

The punch list is a walk-through of the completed work by you, your contractor, and the architect. This is your opportunity to have minor items completed or repaired or replaced. The list of items that could be a problem is endless, but common sense goes a long way. Check all painted areas for even coats and cracks. Check all wood, tile, and stone surfaces for cracks, chips, and stains. Open and close all doors and windows and screens for operation. Check all drains and faucets for leaks and proper water flow. Check carpeting and any cloth finishes for color variations, snags, seams, and stains. In general, when you are standing in a room, imperfections should not be readily visible. It's important after the punch list to set up a schedule to complete the work, although reordering certain materials can cause additional delays.

Warrantees

You should make a one-year labor and a one-year material warrantee by the contractor part of your contract. In addition, items such as roofing, carpeting, appliances, and windows typically have a warrantee from the manufacturer. Fill out the warrantee cards and mail them to the manufacturer. Carpets can fade in sunlight and may need to be replaced. Thermal windows may also need to be replaced due to hazing. Manufacturers who are well known and have national distribution have a vested interest in standing behind their products. Warrantees for furnaces and appliances are important. In the event the product has faulty or dangerous parts, the manufacturers will be able to notify you and replace the parts or correct the problem.

Perry Peterson is a construction supervisor with Mark B. Weiss Construction and has been supervising construction projects for more than 20 years.

7

Influencers and Contacts

Helping people will not guarantee that they respond in kind. My experience is that you can count on about one in ten, but this one makes up for the others.

David Mahoney

One of my favorite friendship quotes comes from Laurence J. Peter, author of *The Peter Principle.* "You can always tell a real friend: when you've made a fool of yourself, he doesn't feel you've done a permanent job." I have lots of good friends in business, some of them in my own profession. I work well and cordially with an increasingly large group of business associates. And I'm very fortunate to have a small, powerful circle of influencers and contacts. What I'm describing here is a network, one of the most powerful tools at anyone's command.

No one goes it alone, and that's most certainly true in real estate development. Even if it were possible to work with everybody in a hands-off manner, you still have to work closely with an astounding number of individuals, companies, and government entities.

As you build this network and help it evolve, you'll make a lot of friends and get to know an even larger number of associates, contacts, and influencers. They are all valuable. You are also of considerable value to the others in your network. For networking to be effective, it has to be a two-way street for every member of the group.

☞ **SECRET OF A MILLIONAIRE REAL ESTATE DEVELOPER**

20. Create and maintain a healthy network.

Keep in mind that it's not really "your" network. The voluntary association belongs to all the members. The more each one helps out the others, the more successful the group and the individuals within it become. It's a way of magnifying the power of the individual by combining knowledge, skills, experience, and contacts. So, let's assume that you are the proverbial man from Mars passing on Earth as a real estate developer. You know no one on the entire planet. So where do you begin building a network of real estate professionals so you can continue your growth?

This network will pay you exponentially when you need and share referrals.

Get Involved in Your Community

Every community is different, but every community regardless of size has one or more groups of people committed to making that community better. A millionaire real estate developer is an involved person. He or she may be active in the community at large, the business community, a chosen profession, or all of the above. The key is involvement, and while there are numerous reasons for involvement, two top the list. One, it's just the right thing to do. Real estate people are by nature builders who devote their lives to making things better. Building a better community is just an extension of their philosophy and commitment.

Two, being involved is good for business, and that's okay. The more people you meet, get to know, and impress, the more contacts and influencers you'll add to your network. You'll also add a few good friends along the way. People just naturally tend to help out and support people they like, respect, and trust.

Opportunities for community service are everywhere. You really don't have to make much of an effort to find them. Wherever you live, you're near a Rotary Club, a Kiwanis Club, a Lions Club, or any of a number of well-respected civic and service organizations that would love to have you as a member. These groups do wonderful work worldwide and in their own communities. If you're not already involved in one of these organizations, check them out. I think you'll be astounded at the extent of their good works and the unlimited options for community service they provide.

The Boy Scouts, Girl Scouts, the Boys and Girls Clubs, and other youth groups need leadership. You'll meet a lot of great contacts helping build your community's youth as you help build the economy of that community. Someday you'll be providing jobs for those kids. You might even find a potential rising star for your own organization or someone worthy of being mentored. Churches and religious-related service organizations are also available and in need of volunteer workers. It's a great way to serve your faith and build up your network of valuable contacts.

Let me be clear about something. When you get involved in a civic-minded organization, I believe service to the community should be your first priority. Hypocrisy makes a poor foundation for a business career; it soon becomes evident, backfires in the face of its practitioner, and eventually does far more harm than good. That being said, I don't believe that service to community and building a business network are mutually exclusive. There's nothing wrong with benefiting from such service. Just make sure you keep your priorities straight.

Get Involved in Your Profession

I think this is essential and for the same reasons. The involvement of real estate developers with each other is good for the profession and helps build the success of everyone in the profession. And it's good for your business. Not only will you make a lot of contacts who can have a direct and positive impact upon your projects, career, and success, you will earn unlimited opportunities for increasing your knowledge and for self-growth.

Start with the local affiliate of the National Association of Realtors (NAR). Look them up in your local phone directory or log on to the Internet at *www.realtor.com*. NAR also publishes an online magazine, Realtor.org, which is packed with valuable information, news, articles, and features relevant to the industry. Much of the incredible variety of helpful material found there is available even if you're not yet a member.

The core purpose of the organization is "to help its members become more profitable and successful." They do that through an amazing variety of services that include providing current information regarding the industry, educating the membership, providing *Realtor.org* and other publications and printed materials, hosting seminars and expos, lobbying state and federal governments, providing research materials, promoting high ethical standards through a tough Code of Ethics and a range of other services. One of their chief purposes is public, business, and governmental advocacy, acting as a "collective force influencing and shaping the real estate industry."

I cannot speak highly enough about these folks and what they accomplish on a local, state, and federal level. Joining should be one of your highest professional goals.

Join Your Local Chamber of Commerce

Involvement in your local chamber of commerce is obviously involvement in your community, but this organization is so fundamental a building block of business, the business community, and the community at large that I believe it deserves special mention. Joining should be an obvious step, but I'm amazed at the number of people in the real estate business who are not members. If there's one group promoting a healthy local economy, a better infrastructure for development and growth, and improvements in the health, education, and quality of life of a community it's the local chamber of commerce. It's probably the one organization where you can meet the highest number of contacts and influencers who can have an impact on your projects and your career. To pass on getting involved with such a powerful group of local business people is to pass on uncounted opportunities.

Membership alone will bring a number of benefits. Getting involved will bring more. The chamber will have a number of departments and a number of committees within those departments. Each affects the business and the quality of life of your community and provides a great opportunity to (again) serve and build a career at the same time. The contacts you make there will be invaluable throughout your career.

Join Local Sales Contacts Clubs

You find these business groups in large, midsize, and even a few small cities. They're organized around the concept of businesspeople meeting in a social setting to promote business within the membership of the group. In some cases only one member of any one profession is allowed in at one time. There may be, however, divisions within a given industry to provide more variety and opportunity within the group. For example, the real estate industry may be represented by someone in residential, someone else in commercial, and someone else in industrial real estate, a developer, an apartment manager, and so on. Be sure you get all the facts on membership before giving a pass to any particular club. Even if there's another real estate professional in your desired group, you may still qualify for membership.

Building contacts and creating relationships with influencers is at the core of sales contacts clubs. You'll meet a lot of "glad-handers" there, selfish people who join for the sole purpose of boosting their own careers and to heck with everyone else. My experience with these groups is that the more you help someone else, the more you end up helping yourself. Word spreads quickly within the group, and the hypocrites soon find themselves frozen out of any real beneficial contacts. Keep your priorities straight, help your fellow businessman or businesswoman, and you'll be helping your own career the best way you can.

I'm not being overly altruistic here. The whole purpose of the organization is to improve your business, but you achieve that goal best by helping others. As Lou Gehrig said, "You don't get the breaks unless you play with the team instead of against it." I think if you get involved and support that group, you'll find that the group will get involved in supporting you.

Become a Mentor

Being a mentor is one of the most rewarding experiences in life. As you begin your career in real estate you really need a mentor, someone who really knows the ins and outs of the business and who can help steer you through the troubled waters of your early years. As you learn and grow and build that career, start looking for opportunities to become a mentor yourself.

I don't think you'll be lacking in opportunities. Millionaire real estate developers develop a good and wide-ranging reputation. Because word gets around as to who knows the score, people respond. You'll hear plenty of knocking on your door by eager real estate neophytes who need your wisdom and experience. Be sure to answer some of those calls, but I also recommend you adopt a few basic rules.

- Don't mentor too many people at one time. You still have a business to run, and despite all your good intentions, your business remains your number one priority. I recommend mentoring one individual at a time or at least phasing one out as you phase someone else in.
- Stay in touch. Even after they have moved on, your advice and counsel can still prove valuable. Also, as their careers grow, they'll more and more be in positions to return the favor by helping you in your projects.
- In the same vein, remember your own mentors. Always be on the lookout for ways to help those who have helped you.
- Avoid the desire to play puppet master. The person you mentor will inevitably make a number of mistakes, and often this is the only way some people can learn. Offer advice, but resist the urge to take control and start pulling strings. Like a kid learning to ride a bicycle, there's going to be some bruises and scratches along the way.
- Don't hesitate to be tough. You don't want to end up like the cowboy I mentioned in Chapter 3, the tenderfoot who didn't become tough, just miserable. Some relationships will blossom into long-term and deep friendships. Others will remain pleasant and valuable associations. Regardless of the emotions involved, sometimes what they call "tough love" is required. You can be direct without being insulting or harmful. Honesty is always the best policy even if it sometimes carries a sting.
- Keep on mentoring. I know lots of real estate developers who invest a lot of their personal time, even in retirement, mentoring young people in the business. It's one of the most rewarding aspects of their lives.

Give As Well As You Get

This is an essential rule of building and maintaining a network. You must be willing to help others even as you help yourself. Influencers and contacts expect and deserve their own influencers and contacts. You're one of them and it's important that you carry your share of the load in the relationship.

It's easy to pass along a tip or a bit of information that's crossed your desk. Anyone can do that. But someone who is involved in building a career will actively seek out ways to help the other people in the network. Doing so is remarkably easy. You have the opportunity throughout the day virtually every day. All you have to do is remember the people in your network and their needs. If you're ready for it, the knowledge that will prove valuable to someone in your group will present itself. Stay alert. You expect the same thing of everyone else in your network, don't you?

One of the best ways to keep the needs of your contacts and influences in what the advertising people call "top of the mind awareness" is to stay in touch with them. This too is easy and should be part of your regular routine. Here are a few helpful ways to do it.

- Clip stories or articles from the news media that are relevant to your associate's business and drop them in the mail with a friendly note. Nowadays you can do that through e-mail almost instantaneously. You don't have to write a letter or long message either. That might even be considered overkill. Just a simple, "Thought you might find this useful" will do.
- Clip stories or articles that mention your associates and send them with a note of congratulations or a "well done." It's easy to do and it shows that you care and that you're aware of the other person and his or her needs.
- Remember birthdays or other important events. Drop a card in the mail, make a phone call, or e-mail a message appropriate for the occasion.
- When passing through the community where an out-of-town contact lives or works, make a phone call just to say hello. Arrange a breakfast, lunch, or dinner meeting if appropriate and if each of you has the time.
- Every once in a while make a phone just to say hello. Again, you don't have to invest an awful lot of time, and you probably shouldn't unless so invited, but the thought will always be appreciated.
- This may be the most important rule of all—listen. When someone communicates with you, listen to what is said. Read between the lines.

Someone might really need to talk, celebrate an event, or just vent his or her frustration. If you're aware of what's really being said, you'll be in a position to offer the correct advice, issue a warning, offer congratulations, or just provide a shoulder to cry on.

A network is a powerful tool. But like any tool it must be kept in condition at all times. Otherwise it just won't be able to do the job when it's most needed.

A Few Works about Contacts

A contact is virtually anyone you, well, contact. Valuable information comes from all types of sources and not all of them will be chair of the executive committee of the local chamber of commerce. A postal employee might mention that she's just spoken to the owner of a prime building that's about to be put on the market. Your garage mechanic could know of some valuable raw land for sale out near his or her hunting camp. Your barber might have heard of an important zoning change that's in the wind. Equally valuable information could come from your doctor's receptionist, a gardener, a florist, a blue-collar worker, a white-collar entrepreneur, or even someone currently unemployed.

Obviously, some contacts will be more valuable over the long run. These are primarily people in business or government who are in a position to offer you information or services. Bankers, accountants, lawyers, and government bureaucrats will possess this information more often and in greater quantity and detail than barbers, gardeners, or postal workers. Still, I never forget that valuable information comes from people in all walks of life. The way I see it, everyone is a contact.

A Few Words about Influencers

An influencer is someone who, obviously, can influence some aspect of your project, your business success, or your career. This person can be in business, the community, the government, or can even be a retired individual who retains clout in those areas. A millionaire real estate developer finds and cultivates influencers in all areas. You just never know when a friendly word or deed in the right place can be instrumental in achieving your goals.

A warning—don't try to buy or curry favor with influencers. Believe me, by the time someone earns recognition as an influencer, he or she has seen all the tricks in the book. Yes, yes, yes, there are exceptions. I know people in influential positions who can be "bought" for an expensive dinner, or baseball tickets, or some other financial perk. I know people who can be "bought" by flattery. The problem with these folks is they don't "stay bought." They're fickle, unreliable, and they certainly don't have your best interests at heart. The truth be known, they're never bought in the first place. They're just playing you for a sucker so they can grab a freebee. These freeloaders can never be a supportive member of anyone's network. They're too self-absorbed.

A millionaire real estate developer just doesn't play that game. It's unproductive. In fact, it's often counterproductive. As a game, it's just no fun, and you always end up the loser. Real influencers act according to the two reasons mentioned at the beginning of this chapter: it's good for the community or profession, and it's good for business. They're due the respect their position in the civic community, their business community, and their profession has earned. I think you'll find that by showing respect, honesty, your abilities, and your concerns for improving your business and community, you'll earn their respect, too.

I have developed relationships with a few people whom I can call at any time to discuss my challenges and problems and to share resources. These are men and women I respect for their ability to not withhold information. I have found over the years that many people, maybe the not so successful people, but big shots just the same, don't share. Then there are many people comfortable in their own skins who do share. I am one of those people, and I like being around the sharing kind.

In retrospect this may seem like a small deal, but years ago I undertook converting an eight-unit apartment building into condominiums. This was my largest project at the time, and six of the eight condos sold pretty fast. Then I had to move the last two, which were the profit makers of the deal. Both were duplex (two-story units), the largest and most costly. I held these units during the winter of 1995 and into the spring season, actually for a little over a year from the time I closed on the original property. I closed in the spring of 1995, sold units in the summer and fall while doing the construction in less than a year, sold three-fourths of the project, and paid the bank. Not bad, but I was worried just the same.

I called a friend, one of the more successful low-keyed developers I knew. He wasn't a millionaire developer. He was multi-multimillionaire developer. When we meet at a deli and I told him my tale of woe, he chuckled and said, "Everything sells Mark, just give it time." I felt better, and yes, as the spring selling season began, guess what, they both sold. Because this person took time from his busy day to hold my hand, now I find time in my busy day to hold hands, too. Give back; I always try to give back as much as I can.

Secrets of Art Evans

1. Buy the property to be developed at a reasonable price. If you pay too much, the deal may never work.
2. Be properly capitalized because developments often cost more than budget.
3. Be realistic when estimating the duration of the development or rehab time because it is very easy to underestimate the amount of loan interest you budget.
4. Use escrow and title companies for payments to contractors and subcontractors to ensure that there are no liens on the property.
5. Get proper legal advice at each stage of the process.
6. Surround yourself with experienced contractors and advisors who can lend assistance and help you make the right decisions at critical times.
7. Insist on flexible loan arrangements in case the development takes longer and in case you need additional funds.
8. Cutting corners leads to problems such as unhappy tenants or buyers, who complain about your work product, additional legal and other costs, adverse reputation, and municipality problems.

Arthur Evans is a real estate attorney in Chicago with a 25-year history of representing real estate developers, owners, and partnerships.

CHAPTER 8

Evaluating Real Estate

Some people are still unaware that reality contains unparalleled beauties.

Bernice Abbott

Bernice Abbott's rather profound statement about life also applies to the world of real estate development. I don't care where you set up shop, wonderful opportunities exist everywhere. Some of you may have to hunt a little harder, look a little longer, bargain a little more sharply, and crunch the numbers a little more carefully, but the deals are there. So are the dogs.

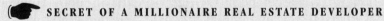 SECRET OF A MILLIONAIRE REAL ESTATE DEVELOPER

21. Know the difference between a deal and a dog of a deal.

Evaluating real estate is a learned skill that sometimes approaches art. I'm not exaggerating. Like artists, we real estate developers look beyond the blank canvas and visualize the unparalleled beauties that can be created within the empty space. In one sense we often have it rougher than artists. Sometimes our canvases are old, ragged, torn, pitted, and full of holes. Yet even then the millionaire real estate developer sees *something,* something of real value there. He or she then sets about making that something happen.

How Real Estate Creates Value

When you buy stocks, mutual funds, options, or other popular investments, you buy at a given price on a given date. Then the price goes up. And then it goes down. And then it goes up and down and up, and the rollercoaster ride has begun. Over time many smart investors have done quite well "playing the market." Others have been wiped out overnight. The stock market is that volatile an investment, and that's one of the reasons I love the more stable arena of real estate development.

Real estate works in a different way and on a different time scale. Over all, it's a much smoother, safer, and more enjoyable ride. Land and property generally hold their value quite well and then over time increase in value until modest investments turn into rather substantial holdings. Real estate generally appreciates on average about 4 percent a year. That's a rule of thumb, and it may not apply to a given development deal. For example, in many of my real estate developments I look for significantly higher rates of growth. It's not unusual to purchase a property, develop it, and turn it at 100 percent of its value. Performing a similar feat in the stock market might be possible, but you sure don't hear of it very often.

Of course, you can experience a bit of the old rollercoaster ride in real estate, too. If you purchase a piece of property without conducting the right amount of research and in the right amount of depth, you could be looking at a stomach-churning, throat-clutching, screaming plummet into the depths of financial ruin.

Generally speaking, real estate maintains its value very well even when the economy turns sour. During the down times some property may not increase in value because there will be less money in the market and fewer deals being made. But the property retains its value. When things start rolling again, and they always do, you won't have to scramble around for opportunities like some of the folks who made other investments. When taking your time to enter the market, real estate is one of the soundest, safest, most profitable purchases you can ever make. Developing that real estate can make it even more profitable.

Value in real estate is as basic as you can get. Somebody has something. Somebody else wants to buy it. A transfer takes place. How much, when, and under what terms all depends on the needs and financial situations of the parties involved. I love that. You never do the same deal twice. It's impossible to get bored in real estate development because each deal will have its own life.

Perception Plays a Role

Much of what we have to deal with in real estate is totally subjective. The market value may have nothing whatsoever to do with a seller's price tag. I've encountered sellers who have refused a fair market price, sometimes a better than fair market price, because of a perceived higher value. That value may be emotional and have little or nothing to do with market realities as seen in the following quotes:

- "I can't sell Mom's house for *that.*"
- "We know that Hilton is putting up a major resort center right next door any day now."
- "You can pay me that amount now, or somebody else will pay it to my grandkids someday down the road."
- "I don't care what your reports say, I know it's worth a lot more!"
- "You can do better than *this!*"
- "Take it. Or leave it."

Sometimes you *can* do better than that, but probably not by as much as the other party wants. This is where your negotiation skills come into play (See Chapter 10). If you're really interested in making this deal happen, use all your skills to make the other party see your point of view. That is to say, try to help him, her, or them look reality in the face. Unfortunately for all concerned, perception can ruin a good deal for all concerned. If they perceive reality as a slap in the face, you're probably better off moving on to a more reasonable seller and situation.

Evaluating Real Estate Is a Team Effort

I believe in teamwork under the leadership of a strong coach who has a goal and a plan. Who makes up that team?

One of your first recruits should be a Realtor and not just any Realtor. Find someone who knows not only the market but that area of the market in which you are most interested. A good Realtor knows the history of your area, its growth patterns, its negative side, and the positive projections for the future. For example, a good Realtor will know, or at least have a "feel" that a prestigious neighborhood is slowly hitting the skids or that a transitional neighborhood is poised for a comeback. He or she will have a better handle on the economic prospects of the community than the average citizen. Most of all a good Realtor is an objective partner in helping get your project off the ground. A good Realtor will be more interested in your long-term success (and his or her long-term success with you, by the way) than in making a quick buck off a sale that is at best marginal for his or her client.

Appraisers and inspectors also are invaluable members of your team. They can spot potential problems and nightmares that most of us wouldn't discover until the panicked phone calls from panicked tenants and the repair bills from numerous suppliers start coming in. The good ones will also alert you to potential treasures that may be hidden to the unpracticed eye, even the unpracticed eye of the current owner. Good inspectors and appraisers also know the quality of work being produced by the suppliers in the community. They should be able to steer you away from the companies practicing shoddy construction and poor business techniques. A building that appears to be in good shape may have been built by a shoddy contractor. Even if the price is right, the maintenance and repairs bills on that property might become a real hindrance to your long-term plans. A good inspector or appraiser can point you to an equally sound deal in a property that is, well, sound. They can also point out the straight arrows in the community and help you establish relationships with quality suppliers you'll need to build and maintain quality properties.

You'll also want to run any serious deals by the other regular members of your business team. Let your lawyer, accountant, and financial advisors take a look at your proposed deal before you commit to anything.

Evaluation Techniques

When it comes to evaluating real estate, I have two recommendations. One, learn enough about the techniques so that you can do a pretty fair job yourself. Two, don't depend on your own skills and experience. In other words, become expert enough to weed out the bad deals, but hire a professional to make sure the selected properties represent good deals. A professional real estate appraiser will see problems and opportunities where you or I might just see brick and mortar, sheetrock and shingle, failure and fatigue, or hope and glory.

There's a big "but" here, and it has everything to do with attitude. An appraiser by his or her very nature is a very practical individual. He or she sees good wood or termite-infested wood. A slab is level or it isn't. The roof will make it through the next rain storm or it won't. A millionaire real estate developer by his or her very nature is a dreamer. We developers see possibilities where others see only practicalities. A negative report may not automatically indicate a negative outcome to our plans. Or our dreams.

How do appraisers go about evaluating property? There are several methods. Here's a sketch of the most popular and practical techniques.

Income Approach

The income approach method of evaluating real estate is based on an estimate of the both the present and future value of that property. What will it be worth next year, the year after, or 10 or 20 years down the road? A basic formula is used to make this calculation.

$$\frac{\text{Expected Annual Income}}{\text{Capitalization Rate}} = \text{Market Value}$$

(The *capitalization rate* is the rate of interest considered to be a reasonable return on investment, given the risk. *Barron's Real Estate Handbook* defines capitalization rate, or cap rate, as a rate of return used to derive the capital value of an income stream.)

Here's how that works. Let's say the property you're considering generates a net operating income of $100,000 annually. Your research into local market conditions indicates a capitalization rate of 10 percent based on the rates of comparable properties in the same area. Using our formula we get the following:

$$\frac{\$100,000}{.10 \ (10\%)} = \$1,000,000$$

Comparable Property Method

As long as we're comparing properties, let's see how we can use some of the same concepts to arrive at a property value. This method uses the value of properties in the same market that are similar in size, age, style, condition, and so on. If a property is valued at X amount, then the comparable property you're considering should be approximately the same or at least within the same ballpark number. For example, if you're buying an apartment building at $450,000 with the same number of units as one just a few blocks away that is valued at $500,000, then your comparable properties should be valued around the same amount, based on prior sales.

Keep in mind that value doesn't always equal the asking price. Your purchase may cost you more because history dictates that property almost always costs less in prior years than today. Those previously mentioned perceptions can still get in your way. A good appraiser takes many factors into consideration. While writing this book, I sold a 63-unit apartment as a sales broker. In order for the appraiser to successfully complete the task of appraising the property, I suggested expanding the geographic area to include properties just a little further out than usual. We looked at larger complexes, smaller complexes, some in better condition and some worse, and weighed the information to accomplish the appraisal using the comparable property method.

Comparative Square Foot Method

While not 100 percent accurate for an appraisal, the comparative square foot method is a good method for getting a reasonably close estimate of value. Let's say you're looking to purchase a 100,000-square-foot building. Find out how much local builders are charging per square foot to put up a structure similar to it. Then multiply that figure times the 100,000 square feet you're considering in order to get your approximate value. You can usually get the average per-square-foot figures with a few phone calls to local builders and contractors in your network.

Cost Approach

This procedure is based on the depreciated replacement or reproduction cost of improvements in the property plus the market value of the site itself. It's not so complicated. For example, let's say the replacement or reproduction cost of a property (the cost of an exact duplication of a piece of property as of a certain date) is $100,000 and the site value is $20,000. Figure the depreciated value (the cost of a property over its useful life), such as these arbitrary figures.

Physical deterioration	$35,000
Functional obsolescence	10,000
Economic obsolescence	5,000
	+ _____
Total accrued depreciation	$40,000

Now let's run the numbers.

Reproduction (new) cost	$100,000
Less depreciated value of improvements	
to the property	− 40,000
	$60,000

Now factor in the site value.

	$60,000
	+ 20,000
Total	$80,000

The value of the property using the cost approach method is $80,000.

The Influence of Expectation

Here's a bit of advice born of personal experience. The realm of science called quantum mechanics involves things on an incredibly small scale, smaller than an atom. Apparently it's quite a different universe down there, and the laws don't always operate the same way they do up here in the land of us big folks. As I understand it, the results of an experiment often are determined by what the experimenter expects to find. For example, if you experiment to determine the nature of light and expect to find a wave, you will find a wave. Your scientific partner who is conducting exactly the same experiment, but who expects to see light as a particle, discovers that light is a particle. Sometimes real estate appraisers appear to be operating under the principles of quantum mechanics.

I've found that often I get the appraised value I expect to get. It's not just me. Other developers, agents, buyers, and sellers experience the same phenomenon. Because appraisers like to make the people who hire them happy, they try to produce the expected results. It's a form of job insurance, I guess. I'm not accusing anyone of being dishonest. Appraisal is, after all, a subjective evaluation. Appraisers just want to do a good job, and part of the definition of a good job includes a satisfied client. Ergo, expected results show up beneath the bottom line on the appraisal form.

This phenomenon doesn't always work in your favor. Sometimes you need a low appraisal, but the other party, the one who hired the appraiser, needs a high value. The situation may be just the opposite, too. My point is that you need to know enough to make a basic evaluation on your own to scout out possible problems and to communicate your thoughts to your own appraiser. Often a second opinion is in order. It makes far more sense to invest in an appraisal than to make a purchase when you have misgivings about the property's value.

This is why it is important for you to develop your own basic skills in real estate appraisal. While a millionaire real estate developer knows his or her job very well, he or she also knows enough of everybody else's job to know when the suppliers are doing their jobs very well, too.

Developing Opportunity Is Right under Your Knows

While teaching a class in Minneapolis in April of 2004, I had a conversation with a student who was taking my class because she was interested in buying and investing in real estate. As we spoke, I asked her where she lived. She told me that she lived in Hudson, Wisconsin, actually a suburb of the Twin Cities. She told me of all the building along Route 94 between Hudson and Minneapolis/St. Paul and how the area in between those two cities was booming. Housing developments, business, and whatever else you think of when you think "developing community" is moving east from the Twin Cities.

Although this person attended my class to learn something new, she knew a lot more than she knew she knew. Without realizing it, she had already conducted a pretty fair initial real estate appraisal, but her expectations got in the way of full realization. When it comes to practical estimating, I suspect you know a lot more than you give yourself credit for.

She had a practical estimate right in her backyard. She could jump on the development train and find a manageable challenge in her area anytime she wanted to. You are the same way. Look in your area. You know the region. Find property in that stable area with growth potential and invest in it. Don't expect sound investments to be located only in certain areas. They're everywhere, and that's where you should be looking, even in your own backyard.

 **SECRET OF A MILLIONAIRE REAL ESTATE DEVELOPER**

22. Look for stable areas with growth potential.

In conclusion, never forget that the world of real estate development really is full of incredible opportunities. Those "unparalleled beauties" can be found in every state of the Union and are available to developers of all sizes, budgets, and interests. The dogs are there, too. That's why millionaire real estate developers invest so much time, energy, and money in learning, performing, and supervising real estate evaluation and appraisal.

CHAPTER 9

Arranging Financing

The deal is only as good as the money the lender brings to the table.

Mark B. Weiss, CCIM

For many years prior to becoming an active observer of real estate developers, I thought successful real estate developing was beyond my capabilities. The cost of the interest every month to carry a project seemed an insurmountable problem. How could developers write a check for the amount of interest due their lender each month while writing even bigger checks to build a highrise? Where did this money come from? Was there a pool of investors willing to pay the thousands or hundreds of thousands of dollars a project would require *in interest alone?* And if such a pool of resources existed, how could I dive in? Well, we don't call this a book of secrets for nothing, and later in this chapter I'll show you the biggest secret available to real estate developers on arranging financing for large projects.

Lenders are in business to do business, and their primary concern is earning a return on their money and rightly so. As we all know, if you don't pay your debt, then your project can fall into default. It's the same as if you failed to make your house or car payments. Sooner or later someone is going to knock on your door and ask for the keys.

Don't panic. Things don't have to work out that way. If you master the secrets of a millionaire real estate developer, they most certainly won't work out that way. Okay, Mark, you ask, how do I put together financing for a real estate development? There are a number of considerations.

First, you will need some initial equity. Any lender will make that requirement. That equity must come from somewhere. It can be real cash from your bank account; from a pooled source of investor money, meaning you, your friends or relatives, or investors; or from a home-equity loan on property you already own or as a second mortgage. Lenders don't want to do business with people who aren't serious about business and finance. Coming up with some of the necessary funds is a way to prove that you are serious about making this deal happen. It's a polite and businesslike way of saying, "Put up or shut up."

If you have large deposits at a local bank, you may be able to use part or all of that equity without actually moving it out of the CD or savings account in which you have placed it. Many lenders will consider such a pledge a satisfactory financial commitment on your part. A lender will require a document committing that equity to the project in case of a default. That's their security for lending you the money.

Depending on the state of the economy at the time you begin your development, a lender may require equity of 20 percent of your costs to acquire and renovate or build the project. That's not a rule set in concrete. Again, depending on conditions, a rate anywhere within the range of 10 percent to 25 percent is possible. When the economy is bustling, the rate may be a combination of 10 percent of the purchase price for the property plus 20 percent of your borrowed costs. For example, if you are buying your property for $100,000 and planning to put $100,000 into it, 10 percent of the $100,000 would be $10,000. Add 20 percent of the cost borrowed to the initial 10 percent, and you would need $30,000 to get the project going.

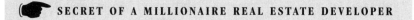

SECRET OF A MILLIONAIRE REAL ESTATE DEVELOPER

23. Always shop for the best loan possible.

Shop around for lenders just as you would shop for a good deal on a house, an automobile, or steaks for the weekend barbeque. Differences may be small, but small differences can add up over time to great advantage. It's important to determine borrowing requirements and any pertinent restrictions or conditions. Rates will vary market to market and even within a given market. Look, you shop around to find the best property, don't you? Doesn't it make good sense to shop around for the best money to make that deal happen? The key variables will always be the current status of the lending institution in your market and how much money they want to put into the streets in the form of construction loans. Notice that these factors are completely out of your control. That means you have to make sure to make the best loan-request presentation possible so that you can get your share of whatever money is available.

It's important to understand the difference between interest rates and the rates lenders offer. Interest rates may not vary that much. If your home mortgage rate is 5 percent in New York, chances are it will be 5 percent in San Francisco and everywhere in between. You may experience a little variation here and there, but even then the rate will be close to that 5 percent. The market on interest rates is pretty stable.

Construction lenders are different and see things by a different light. Their construction loans do not have the same market or tight restrictions that we see in conventional mortgage rates. Some lenders who require 10 percent equity on the whole deal charge a higher interest rate on construction. This rate could be as high as 12 percent for a first-time borrower. Other lenders may charge you 2 points or 2 percent of the deal as an upfront fee with a low interest rate. It's a free market, folks, and like the old saying about the golden rule always applies: they who have the gold rule.

Risk and reward fall hand in hand. Risk to the lending institution is the guaranteed reward to the lending institution for taking that risk. Of course, they're counting on that risk to pay off—with interest, so to speak. Because every lender is different, every lender has different policies and procedures. Again, it is important to shop, shop, shop, shop to get the best deal. Bear in mind that large institutions like multinational banks or multistate banks may choose not to deal with the small borrower. From their point of view, the time invested in putting together a small construction loan will yield a smaller profit than the same amount of time invested on a loan for a multimillion dollar project. You can't blame them. Well, you can, but it won't do you a lot of good. Like the rest of us, lenders just want to make the best, most profitable deals they can.

When you are starting out and haven't built a track record, sometimes you have to pay a higher fee at a higher point. Those are just the rules of the game. Accept it as part of your tuition to gain practical experience. Realize also that your creditworthiness will change rapidly as your real estate development career succeeds. Your leverage will only come from the experience that you develop through your successful projects.

Understand What Financial Institutions Want

Financial institutions are primarily interested in two things in a borrower: a good reputation from a solid track record and equity to fund a deal so they can feel confident of a return on their money. Let's take a very basic view at how lending institutions work. Money is lent at an interest rate with additional fees to the bank. The rate plus the fees is higher than the rate paid to depositors who have money in the institution. Lenders want to make sure that they get their depositors money back with a good rate of return—profit. To achieve that from real estate developers, any loan that is deposited to your bank must be underwritten. That means it will be presented to and analyzed by a group charged with that responsibility. The "group" may be a committee or just a single person, but regardless the loan will have to go to a loan committee for approval.

To submit your loan to an institution for financing, you will need to provide them with your tax returns and financial statements. This we can take for granted, but, as they say on the game shows, "But wait, there's more." You'll need to step above and beyond making a submission to make a presentation in person. The presentation must include the projections and financial outcome of the real estate development project you plan to undertake.

In each case you will need to provide

- the property address,
- the unit mix,
- a physical description,
- the acquisition price,
- a construction budget showing the amount of money you want to borrow, and
- a financial breakdown of your project.

Borrowed money can be used for a variety of improvements. Rather than list the multiple examples of what those improvements could be here, I'd like you to refer to the budgets in Appendix B.

Figure the Cost of Interest

In addition to the money you are borrowing, you need to figure in the cost of interest to carry the project. Based on prevailing rates, interest should be calculated at a rate that will allow you the time to buy and close your property and obtain your zoning and permit approvals. You'll need to factor in time to sell or lease the property because even when you are finished with your project you will be paying interest on your loan until the property is sold, closed, and your lenders are paid off.

To determine the cost of interest, use this formula. It's always worked well for me. Take the aggregate price from your acquisition and hard costs and multiply by the percentage rate you earn. For example, let's say you are buying a property at $100,000 and spending another $100,000 on maintenance and repair. That equals $200,000. The interest rate you can get is 6 percent, which means you pay $12,000 per year (6 percent × $200,000). You may not spend all that you borrow, but it's a smart move to have more money on hand than you think you'll need.

SECRET OF A MILLIONAIRE REAL ESTATE DEVELOPER

24. Always borrow more money than you believe you'll need.

When I began in real estate development I tried to work on a very tight budget. I didn't calculate additional interest cost or money needed to finish a project. As a result I was under budget and felt humiliated when I had to ask for more money. The embarrassment soon went away when I realized that I wasn't the only one making this mistake. The more difficult problem in the transaction actually came when the lenders said that they were charging additional points and fees to rewrite the loan and that there would be delays related to submitting it back to underwriting. So to avoid the additional costs, fees, and delays involved in putting together the additional loan, always ask for more money than you actually need. You may pay more in initial points, the percentage up front that each lender charges to lend you the money, but the difference between 1 percent of $100,000 and 1 percent of $90,000 is only $100. The $100 that you will pay in points frees up $10,000 more dollars for your project if you need the money. That is a lot less expensive than taking the time, effort, and cost to apply for a revised construction loan. It is important to have those funds lined up so your project can move on quickly and easily. Frugality is an admirable trait, but not when it starts costing you money, time, and a good night's sleep.

Even in the best of times you have to give yourself an adequate period to start, finish, sell, and close or lease up. Everything takes longer than you think. Always give yourself more time than your lender might initially suggest.

There are problems with lending institutions even when they are quick to underwrite loans. I have never had a lender who has looked at my proposal to come back to me and make realistic suggestions on how to make the deal work better or to plug the holes that I may not have seen. I have had lenders who have for a variety of reasons rejected a loan application because it didn't fit their lending standards or criteria at the moment. I have had more lenders make loans happen without ever offering a critical analysis. You would think that as an advisor on the money they are lending they'd make this effort.

Early in your career you may expect a lender to act as a security blanket. We think they would look at our numbers or projections and then say to us: "Do you need to include more time to finish the project?" Or, "You are not taking into consideration certain construction expenses that we believe important," or some other sound recommendation. But it just doesn't happen, at least in my experience. It seems that the lenders are always either too critical or they're not critical at all.

When I started in this business, I thought that my lender was going to be more or less of a watchdog over my interests. Certainly they will lend me money, but I thought that when I submitted a proposal to a lender for a real estate development deal that they might actually analyze it, fine tune it, and come back to me with suggestions to make the deal better. That was the situation in just one case. In every other case my lenders just approved whatever I submitted, which, in retrospect, was quite dangerous for each of us. They should have been more careful with their own money, but I should have been more careful and more savvy in asking for some of it. I learned the hard way once in the deal that I needed more money, or that my projections for future rents or sales may have been overly optimistic.

Developing real estate is really a financial matter that takes a lot of time and energy from the developer. You have to come out with more money than you started with. Certainly we know that is a very simple concept, but what kind of cost did you not take into consideration? What are you forgetting about? What unexpected nightmares could come out of the darkness? What vital information are you lacking? Here is where a good lender comes into the equation, especially when you are new to the business. A good lender will show you what you have left out of your equations. But that's not something you can count on. It's always best to cover your own bases.

Lenders get paid a percentage, or a point, for placing the loan with a specific institution. This can vary from $\frac{1}{2}$ a percent to 3 percent depending on your market and your area. The lender's concern and commitment is more for their commission than it is to get you into a sound economic situation. These are businesspeople, and their business is making money off money. Never forget that when dealing with them. Your interests are always secondary to them.

During the financial interview process, look for an interested party who will give you constructive criticism based on experience. This may sound odd, but you really don't want someone who will just "rubber stamp" an approval on your loan just to get a mortgage broker fee or a point. That approval may okay a project with serious and costly defects. Fortunately real estate development allows room for error. I have experienced a number of situations in which I was overly optimistic or didn't take into consideration the reality of time or the expense of money or the errors of contractors along the way and I have still landed on my feet.

Three Strikes, but I Wasn't Out

My first attempt to convert a building to condominiums ended up better in ways I initially never considered. In this example I hope that you will learn some of the things that can go wrong and that things can still turn out right in the end. I found an apartment property in the Sheridan Park neighborhood of Chicago's north side, north of Wrigley Field, which was just beginning a gentrification. The owner passed away, and the lender decided to exercise "a due on death clause." This means that if a borrower dies, the lender can call the note that is due upon the death of the borrower. The building had never had a late payment in its entire mortgage. The property was managed by a reputable firm, yet the lender decided to make life miserable for the heirs to the estate by putting them up against a foreclosure time clock with the due upon death clause.

I was appointed receiver by the court and given responsibility to run the property. It had recently been renovated and although some work was required to bring it up to condo quality, it was a beautiful building with a lot of promise.

There were ten units; six were one bedroom, one bath, large units of approximately 750 square feet. Four of the units were two bedrooms with a den, dining room, kitchen, and large living room. The building was a prize with a terrific bonus, 14 parking places for 10 units.

I had never done a conversion before, but I had seen other developers do it. My initial thought was to create six glorious units out of the ten existing units. What do I mean specifically? Well, the first floor of the building had two one-bedroom units on both the east and west side. My grandiose plan was to combine those and the garden unit, thus "duplexing" these units to create four-bedroom, three-bath units. I knew I'd get a higher price than a one-bedroom unit would sell for. The tenants who were living in the two-bedroom-with-den units were using them as three-bedroom units. I thought I would sell four three-bedroom units, thus having six units at the high end of the price scale and be successful in my first development.

I created a model in one of the larger units using a contractor who had just done some work for me in my home. Here is where the challenge came in. The property was scheduled for foreclosure, so I had to go to a lender who could lend me the money while we were playing beat the clock. A lender I had just completed a real estate brokerage deal with said they could close quickly, within a week or two. They were even ready to do an appraisal after the fact. That's highly unconventional, but they knew the value would be justified. They felt that they had a safety net with respect to what I was paying.

They were not going to charge me any points for the loan, but they were going to charge me a $3,000 release fee for every unit. Six times $3,000 is $18,000. This was my first development. The market was in the middle of the savings & loan debacle of the early 1990s. Banks were closing, and even experienced developers were not able to get money for deals. It was a tough time, believe me. I knew a small savings & loan where I had placed a large construction loan for a brokerage client. I knew they charged a high rate, but I also knew they could and would close deals quickly, so that had value. I had to sell my financial soul to the lender, though, to get the deal done.

Knowing that the time clock was ticking, I had no alternative. I signed on the dotted line, the money came to the table, and I closed. My first wrong move was overpaying for money. I mean I way overpaid for money. My second wrong move, when my lender approved my loan, was to agree to pay interest every month out of pocket. Then I made a third wrong move by underestimating how much money I'd need to fix up the building. In baseball, "three strikes and you're out." Thank goodness real estate development can be more flexible than baseball.

Once I had the building in hand, I began to contact some of Chicago's more successful real estate brokers. I wanted their opinion on my idea of what to do when capitalizing my first development. At the time, people were making money hand over fist converting buildings to condominiums, and I was quite excited about my prospects. I was suffering from the same affliction that many people in real estate face—greed. I wanted a piece of that big pie that seemed so easy to bake. I walked brokers through the property. They set up appointments for me to look at other duplex units, big units in the community. They confirmed my thoughts as to what to build on the site. Not one told me my idea for this project was off base. I met a lot of "yes men" and "yes women" who supported my fantasy.

And that was wrong step number four, listening to bad advice. They were all wrong. The project never sold a unit. I had vacated the building, fixed up a model, made the monthly payments, but nothing happened. Why didn't the property sell? Because most people will buy a one-bedroom or a two-bedroom unit, and we were marketing three and four bedrooms. We missed the market completely. There's a lesson to be learned here, and it's the next secret.

 **SECRET OF A MILLIONAIRE REAL ESTATE DEVELOPER**

25. Sell what you own, don't change what you own.

Had I tried to sell six one-bedroom units at the lowest end of the pricing spectrum, they would have blown out the door and turned a solid profit. If I had recognized that a two-bedroom with den was not a three-bedroom unit, those would have blown out the door as well. Hundreds of people came to look at our project. The amount of time I and my staff invested seemed endless, but nothing popped. I consulted with a few more real estate professionals who confirmed my thoughts. I began to realize a need for a change.

By the end of the summer of 1993, I had decided to hire a property management company. I handed them the keys and told them to call me in a year. They immediately leased the property and were able to fill it with tenants. I went to another lender and refinanced the existing debt. At that time, I had to pay that $18,000 release fee to lender number one because they were getting their points at the back end of the deal. The economics were that the building cost me initially $420,000. The points added another $18,000. Nine months of interest added another $35,000. Renovation costs were $50,000. The amount of money down was $80,000, which came out of my own pocket. Three years later I finally sold the property. Fortunately the condominium situation had failed. I say fortunately because when I sold the building I was able to experience the government's 1031 rule. This bit of legislation allowed reinvesting the money into other buildings rather than treating my money as ordinary income.

I eventually sold the property for $895,000. After brokerage commissions, I had $850,000 thousand dollars. I paid off my $480,000 mortgage and used the balance to acquire three more buildings. From those buildings, I sold one or two over the years and started growing exponentially toward building a strong portfolio. Despite all the bad advice from the "geniuses" in lending, brokerage, architectural firms, and everyone else, I came out all right on the deal.

Regardless of how many geniuses you talk to, you have to have your own sense of what you are doing. The bottom line is basic. You can't blame anyone other than yourself for bad decisions. Ultimately you always call the shots. People who have interviewed me after reading books I've written on other real estate topics sometimes do not like my suggestions. They'd rather jump right in and rush the shopping around and doing your homework phase of real estate development. The ones who survive in this business will eventually learn. Please read, study, and understand the information in this book. What I am telling you won't be taught in school. You need experience. Take one year before you do anything and go into the field and observe, observe, observe, and then realize that you are still going to make mistakes. You'll want the money to do your deal, and you'll have to jump through a lot of hoops for the lenders to get it. Even then it is essential that you cover all your bases. Apply some critical analysis to guide you and to keep you from making costly and humiliating mistakes.

Assemble a Professional Presentation

In developing a professional presentation, it is important for you to have your numbers in order, to check and double-check the equations, and to know the market for your product. The best market analysis you can get is from interviewing real estate brokers and looking in the multiple listing service for your targeted community. This is part of that homework I keep insisting you do. If you are looking at renovating a house or a condo, or want to build apartments, you do need accurate statistical information, including hard data or current and projected pricing.

A local Realtor can be your best friend in this regard. They have up-to-the-minute information as well as historical data that is critical to your becoming a successful developer. In fact, experienced Realtors who have represented many new and experienced developers have a wealth of knowledge to share. They know what is offered in the market as standard items and features by competitors. They know what works and doesn't work. They know what others have done to make a project successful. More than that, their income is directly related to your success. Like others you will have on your team be sure you check the experience level of the Realtors you choose.

One big problem that people create for themselves is letting their ego drive their business. Millionaire real estate developers may have big egos. It often comes with the territory, but they don't let their emotions dictate business decisions. For example, in the past few years we have seen the use of granite counters, stainless steel appliances, and very expensive packages used to attract people to buy property. This is especially true in urban areas. The developer can brag about using "only the best" and "top of the line" materials. Yet that is not what every buyer is looking for, and pricey extras certainly do not always bring you the return on your investment you need. White-on-white appliances and counters that are not stone tops are a wiser financial investment and one appreciated by most consumers especially in starter residential projects.

If you are selling condominiums or homes in the half-million-dollar-price range, you may need to have luxury items, amenities, and upgrades you won't find in starter homes and starter projects. Whatever you do must always be economically feasible. If you build just for the sake of building, don't expect to make any money.

👉 **SECRET OF A MILLIONAIRE REAL ESTATE DEVELOPER**

26. Every element of every real estate development project must have a financial justification.

Don't misunderstand me. If you want to let your ego make a decision, that's your business. Just make sure you realize there's a price to pay and you'll be the one paying it.

If you are going build a small shopping center or a leased investment, certainly you should consult with experts in the marketplace. I recommend that you consult with people who have earned a CCIM, Certified Commercial Investment Member, designation. As you know, I've earned that designation and speak from experience. To get those four letters behind your name, you need to invest 200 hours of graduate-level study. Combined with the professional real-world experience required, this is the best real estate education you can get. Of all the real estate professionals around, only 7,000 of us have earned the right to put CCIM on our letterheads. These people know real estate. They're market experts and can help you with your own analysis or with getting a property under control and stabilized. Go to CCIM.net to find a list of our designees. Look for the professionals in your area, and look at their resumes to choose the specialization in the category of development you are doing.

Having information from your experts in your file when you put together your presentation package is crucial. Someone told me that when presenting information, it should always be brought down to the lowest common denominator. If the material is too complex and difficult for people to understand, their lack of understanding works against you no matter how well you are able to grasp details and complex concepts.

The elements you want to include in your presentation are:

- Your experience
- Your architect
- Property zoning
- Property survey
- Your plans for the property
- Budget
- Projected development chronology
- Ultimate leasing or sale prices
- Anticipated profit

You should also include an exit strategy, noting that you intend to refinance the property, input an end loan (a mortgage), or sell the units if the project involves attached homes or condominiums. The full scope—from beginning to middle to end—needs to be included. You should begin putting together your own pro forma very early. Start out in the roughest and most simplified way so that you can explain it and anyone who hears your presentation can understand it. The thinking processes involved and the practice will do you good.

When presenting to your lender or to investors for that matter, your presentation package will be extremely helpful, and this early work makes for a good outline of your project. In addition to the aforementioned items and parties, you should emphasize the high quality of work of your list of contractors and referrals. Include all the information in a nice complete package. Include everything that you need so that the project actually makes sense to your audience and so you can explain it to your lender in a very brief period of time.

Brevity in presentation is a skill you should master. Often a few organized and well-spoken words can accomplish more than a long, rambling, and confusing speech that loses its audience in detail and complexity. The brief time available with your lender may simply be just that, a few minutes of their valuable time. The presentation may be made in a conference room, in your office, or even in your home. Whatever the environment, you need to know your material and have the ability to present it clearly, concisely, and with conviction. You want the lender to walk away with some of that conviction. The use of a digital camera to build a presentation on your laptop computer is a great idea. Actually taking your lender or investors on a tour of the neighborhoods, similar development, and the property you are intending on developing is a great time saver in the presentation process.

Sometimes when presenting you may want to have another expert with you, such as your architect, construction supervisor, or your Realtor. I've found that other professionals can lend authority to my presentation, especially when they are good presenters and can make a logical case for the proposal. You don't need to spend hundreds of thousands of dollars in putting together your presentation, but your presentation does need to be organized, professional, and easy to understand. You want to share the vision and the passion you have for your project, backed up with the necessary facts and figures.

How to Make Interest More Interesting

Here's a great secret shared by millionaire real estate developers. Remember, earlier in this chapter I mentioned why I never thought I'd be a real estate developer. I was intimidated by the huge monthly interest payments required by lenders. I discovered something very interesting after doing my first real estate development. Smart developers don't write an interest check every month.

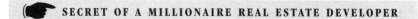

SECRET OF A MILLIONAIRE REAL ESTATE DEVELOPER

27. Use an interest reserve.

An interest reserve is simply the amount of interest due on your loan, but it is budgeted monthly. It is a budget item that the lender contributes each month tacked on to the debt that you owe the lender. In other words, if you borrow $1 million and your interest is $5,000 a month, after the first month you owe the lender $1,005,000. At the end of the second month you owe $1,010,000, at the end of the third month it is $1,015,000, and so on, and so on. I call this invisible money, You never touch it, but its there all right. It is budgeted into the project cost and comes out of the lenders pocket not yours. Remember, interest reserve is your best friend in making a deal happen. It also makes the lender successful. Remember, lenders make their money on interest. They bill you for it and you pay it. Your key to success is always doing your projections correctly. Too much interest can kill the profit in a deal, especially during times of rising interest rates.

If you listen carefully, you can almost hear the interest clock ticking. Do you hear it? It is always ticking away. When interest rates are increasing, and they at some time always will increase, this is a very loud tick-tock. When things are humming along fine, the tick-tock is less intrusive. When your sales or leasing projects are taking too long, this clock is overbearingly loud.

SECRET OF A MILLIONAIRE REAL ESTATE DEVELOPER

28. Beware the interest clock.

When you refinance or pay off your lender, that's when they get paid from the advance of the interest reserve that has supported your project financially over the months. When you see Donald Trump or similar high-profile developers building $100,000,000 and $200,000,000 developments in prime areas throughout the country, understand that they are certainly not writing interest checks every month. They figure into their budget the interest reserve that will be repaid to the lender when the project is complete. A millionaire real estate developer never goes out of pocket after the day the loan closes. All funding for every expense comes from the lenders. The more the lenders have invested in a deal, the more of a partner they are because their investment will not let them abandon the property.

Take Care of Yourself As Well As Your Suppliers

Here is another secret you will learn only in this book. "How do I get paid during the development?" That's a big question, and I hear it a lot from people just beginning their careers. Developer fees are the funds that pay you for doing your own project; they should be figured in when doing your presentation. Developer fees can't be overly generous, but they should be reasonable and fair to compensate you for your time and effort on a monthly basis, or other reasonable time period, for the amount of time and effort that you put into your project. Whether you pay yourself every month or whenever you go in for a construction draw, make sure that you are paid for your hard work. When I started out, I thought it only fair for me to get paid at the end of the deal, to be paid from the profits. That sounds reasonable, right? Sorry, it was wrong.

The first project I completed worked out successfully, and I deferred my compensation until the end of the deal. I just thought that was the moral and proper thing to do. I didn't treat business as business. Do as I say, not as I did. Whenever you see developers living like kings and the property isn't finished, understand that they are paying themselves to be builders. Fortunately I had income and revenue sources that supported me during the time I worked on my transaction but wasn't earning anything from that transaction. Now I realize I deserve to be paid as much as the next guy, and as often as the next guy, and there is nothing wrong with that. In fact, that is the norm.

When I began, I thought borrowing money was a privilege. I thought deferring my compensation until the end of the deal was my responsibility.

I also believed I was privileged to overpay for everything because of the opportunity that these generous lenders were providing to me. Little, old me without experience soon began to learn things the hard way. Over time I realized that the only person I had to be generous to was me. Lenders come and go. Someone else is always available to lend you money. It is critical to figure into your budgets all of your costs so that you don't fall short, that you figure in a length of time that you feel is most reasonable to do to complete your project as well as all other time frames and costs that are going to make your life easier. And be sure to figure in an appropriate amount of money for yourself to draw during the length of the project.

Construction Draws and What They Mean

Renovations and development require the regular borrowing of money throughout the length of the project. In structuring the deal, it is important to know that financing comes in three categories. The first is your acquisition loan, the second is the money arranged for financing to carry the project, and the third is the construction money to complete the project.

The construction loan element is critical because that's where it will take some real input on your part to make sure that your applications towards money and construction draws begin once you have your contractors budgets in place and you are viewing the progress of their work. For instance, if you have a 12-month project, you have a 12-month budget, and it is quite simple to realize that you are going to pay it out in 12 monthly increments. The increments may vary from month to month. During the middle of the project you will probably pay out more as your project progresses. At the end, when things taper down, you pay off minimal amounts to finish the job.

Regardless of the time frame required to initiate your construction project, you will need to apply to your bank regularly for money to finance your development. These are called construction draws and must be part of your financial agreement. They usually begin with an "application for advance" to your bank or title company.

You will list each of your contractors separately by name and by trade on the application for advance. Next to their name you will include the amount of their contract. In the column next to that, you will include payment to date. For example, if you have a contractor who gives you a bid of $20,000 to do tiling, the first column will list ABC Contractors and tiling, the second column will list contract amount of $20,000, the third column will be the amount paid to date whatever that amount may be. The fourth column will be the balance due. The next column is called "retention." To keep contractors in line, it is customary to retain 10 percent of their payouts to make sure that they finish the job. If your initial tile contractor is requesting $2,000, they will really end up getting a payment of $1,800, and you will add in your retention column $200 or 10 percent of whatever your monthly payment is.

That's your insurance that the company or individual will complete the job. Sadly, it is not unusual to have a contractor fail to finish his or her work. It's an unpleasant thought, but it's also an unpleasant reality. The money you have retained will have to be used to pay someone else to come in and finish that job. There is an example in the Appendix B for your review.

These forms get submitted not just to the bank requesting the dollars that you are looking for but also to the title company. The title company will make sure that no liens are placed on the property before they protect the lender and release the forms to you. When you apply for your application for advance, it is critical to get lien wavers from your contractors. These documents provide that your contractors have actually been paid their money and are waiving their right to lien the property based upon work and services provided.

A lien is a charge against a property that makes the property security for the payment of a debt, judgment, taxes, and so on. If you do not get the waivers, it is possible that the contractor could claim you haven't paid your bills. The company could get a lien against your property and stall, sabotage, or even ruin the project. The waivers of lien that you must require and request with every payout must encompass two areas. The first is a partial waiver of lien as your contractors are receiving partial payments. It is important that you keep these for your records to show that people have been paid. Second, when the final payment is made, they receive a final waiver of lien indicating a lien that has been paid in full.

In summary, don't be intimidated by the prospect of acquiring the money you need for your projects. It's there and it's available, even if you do have to jump through a lot of hoops to get it. The real key is getting enough money and allowing yourself enough time to complete the development. Don't forget, you'll need more of each than you believe when you start out. Plan accordingly, and the money the lender brings to the table will do the job.

Real Estate Development Secrets from Ben Weiss

The seven most important secrets and considerations in making a real estate deal work are as follows:

1. Pay the best acquisition price. In most deals the profit is made on the purchase price.
2. Determine your proposed use for the property in the beginning.
3. Choose the right location for your specific use. This must be right for your use.
4. Create a quality team that includes the following (not necessarily in the order presented):
   - Architect
   - Builder/Contractor
   - Managing Agent/Broker
   - Accountant
   - Lawyer
5. Fix a time table/schedule. Set it up and stick to it especially during periods of high interest rates.
6. Advertise but don't overadvertise. That's money down the drain because the market moves at its own pace.
7. Be upfront with investors. Get adequate capital in your initial offering. It is a difficult obstacle to go back to your original investors and ask for more money latter.

Ben Weiss has been developing property in Chicago since 1959 and is one of the founding members of the Lincoln Park Builders Club of Chicago.

CHAPTER 10

The Art of Negotiation

Say no, then negotiate.

Anonymous

Everyone Should Be a Winner

I began this chapter with what I consider a negative quote because I believe it brilliantly expresses a serious problem with the way we Americans negotiate business these days. We approach it as if going to war. We seem to be obsessed with beating the other guy to a pulp as seen in the following remarks.

- "We sure whipped 'em that time, boss."
- "We creamed 'em, didn't we?"
- "They couldn't handle what we threw at 'em."
- "I knocked 'em dead."
- "Like lambs to the slaughter!"
- "They went *down!*"

Don't get me wrong. I believe in and certainly enjoy winning any negotiation. I do my best to come out on top, but there's a significant difference in focus between winning and knocking 'em dead. I hope you can see that difference or that this chapter helps you realize that most significant point.

Winning is a positive goal. Beating someone to a pulp is a negative and misdirected goal. As long as I achieve my goals in a negotiation, I don't care how well the other guy does. Ideally, he or she will leave the negotiation feeling as good as I feel about it. I have seen hundreds of cases where someone beat, creamed, or knocked someone down in a negotiation and still came out a loser in the long run. In fact, the biggest losers I know always behave poorly in negotiating. I like win/win situations. Someone's real personality comes out when they behave poorly. Listen to and observe carefully such behavior. You'll learn a lot more than the other person wants you to learn.

I talked to someone who judged a collegiate-level, regional competition among advanced marketing students. Teams from three universities made the finals, and two of those schools were long-time and bitter rivals. When the winners were announced the chairman of the judging committee said, "Well, College B, you came here to beat College C. And you did." There were cheers and high-fives from the College B team and frowns and sighs from the other. Then the judge continued, "But first place goes to College A because it made the superior presentation." Get it? College B achieved their goal of beating their rival, but another team took home the big prize because they had their priorities straight. The difference between winning and beating may be subtle, but it's a difference that can make you a millionaire real estate developer instead of a second-place finisher.

I never pay sticker price for an automobile. Would you buy a house without making a counteroffer to the seller's listed price? When buying something, haven't you ever asked a salesperson, "Can you help me on this?" Even deciding where to spend the family vacation can involve debating techniques, give and take, threats, pleading, dirty tricks, and bribery that would make UN negotiations seem pale by comparison. Everything is a negotiation, and that is especially true in real estate development. You'll negotiate hourly rates, flat

---

SECRET OF A MILLIONAIRE REAL ESTATE DEVELOPER

29. Even when you come out on top, negotiate win/win scenarios.

fees, costs, and percentages not once but again and again throughout your career. If you're to succeed at becoming a millionaire real estate developer, you'd better learn the art.

How to Deal with the Four Personality Types

Negotiation is all about communicating effectively with people, and there are all kinds of people. Every situation is unique and will bring its own set of challenges and opportunities. People are the same way. No two are alike. That being said, just about everyone you meet in any area of life will fall into one of four basic personality types. I label them the brain, the pusher, the friend, and the artist. When you read other books on negotiation (And you will, won't you?), you may see them identified as the analytical, driver, relator, and socializer, and other writers have offered different labels. They all describe the same things. It's important that you understand these personality types and identify them in the people with whom you work. If you want to win your negotiations, you'll have to adjust your approach to one that is appropriate for each type. Here's a brief look at what these folks are like.

The Brain

A *brain* is a cautious person with a focus on acquiring accurate information before taking any action. Often, this quest for information gets in the way of actually coming to a conclusion, making a final decision, and taking action. Because these people like to get things right, they're always asking for more information, data, reports, and feedback. You'll find them to be "control freaks," but inwardly directed. They do not like risk taking, and dealing closely with risk-takers may give them a case of the negotiating "willies."

On the positive side, they plug away and are determined to solve whatever problem they face. When given a firm deadline, they'll make it although their need for data may drive you to distraction during the process. They are serious, organized, and interested in making sure the processes they're involved in work well. They're not comfortable operating "outside the box" of corporate or business structure, but within official guidelines they make good problem solvers.

They don't react well to emotional outbursts or actions they perceive as irrational. The "touchy-feely" approach doesn't work well with a brain. A pat on the back or a hug is uncomfortable. Overly friendly chats about family, hobbies, sports, or whatever get in the way of getting the job done. So does any overly emotional display in a business environment. They believe conflict is to be avoided at all costs if at all possible.

When working with a brain, remember that he or she needs to understand the process of what's going on, organization, structure, lots of information, time to do the job right, and a friendly, but hands-off relationship. When I have observed people in this category, they react too slowly and lose deals. Most work for others and are not entrepreneurs.

The Pusher

A *pusher* is a take-charge personality, someone who likes to jump in, run the show, get things done, and move on to the next challenge. Pushers focus on achieving a clearly-stated goal in the most efficient, most productive, and most profitable manner. Many of society's overachievers are pushers. The adage "if you want to get something done, give it to a busy person" was written about a pusher. They like to handle multiple tasks at the same time. And they're very good at it.

Pushers are outwardly directed control freaks who really like to run the show and everyone in it. They're competitive and aren't shy about insisting that they get the authority to finish the job at hand. They move fast, act fast, and lose interest fast. This can be a real problem because when they lose interest they may just drop whatever project they're working on and move on to another. Sudden changes won't usually throw them, and they'll probably enjoy the new challenge. A lot of the independent contractors you work with will have pusher personalities.

The good news is that they'll push hard to get the job done on time and on budget. The bad news is they'll kick and scream all the way. They're so focused on getting the job done that they may not hear you when you speak. Their minds are probably off solving one of your problems or a problem on another job site or for another client. Make sure that a pusher is actually listening whenever he or she appears to be hearing what you say. And never let them push you to discomfort in a transaction. You are the captain and must have control. Can you imagine Donald Trump being pushed by a member of his staff?

The Friend

A *friend* will be a "people person" who enjoys the social aspects of business relations and who puts a priority on personal relationships. Their "go along to get along" philosophy makes for smooth relationships, but it can cause problems. In an attempt to avoid conflict, a friend may also avoid bringing up unpleasant subjects or bad news. As a real estate developer, bad news is the kind of information you need to get as quickly as possible.

Friends are security conscious and are slow to make decisions. They also seek comfort in a large network of friends and associates. Unlike a thinker, who wants a lot of information before making a decision, a friend wants to know what everybody else thinks. Consensus is important, and sometimes the quest for agreement can impede their progress in attaining a goal. They are good workers, supportive of the cause, and make excellent team players. In fact, being within a team is their comfort zone. Risk-taking out there on their all by themselves is not their forte.

They are sensitive people and may take criticism of job performance personally. Friends will require lots of data on your project, a personal relationship, a lack of conflict, and a sense of achieving success through group action.

My observation of these people is that they have a very hard time conducting serious business. Because they need and want to be liked, they cannot behave in a businesslike manner, confronting, issuing to, and directing other people. In a social setting one would never ask business questions as they would be crossing the social norms. Questions such as "How much money do you have to invest?" would be inappropriate, but in business you must ask money questions, many money questions. Despite what the friend may believe, such questions aren't personal. They're just business.

The Artist

An *artist* is someone who enjoys life, even on the job. They're friendly, open, direct, and supportive of mutually agreed on goals. They are full of energy, enjoy being active, and always want to be at the center of that action. You'll find them very enthusiastic about any of your projects with which they're involved. But because they have a short attention span, you'll have to make an effort to keep them on track.

The "touchy-feely" approach, the slap on the back, the hug, and other shows of affection work well and are appreciated by the artist personality. Artists like and will respond well to an appreciative audience, even an audience of one. They're not detail-oriented people and may often take the fly-by-the-seat-of-my-pants approach to a given project.

When working with an artist, you'll most likely have to help get them organized and to stay organized through completion of their portion of your project. Insist on accuracy in any documentation, reports, or paper work and then expect to double-check what data you can on your own. Remember the importance of social interaction and the emotional side of the relationship in any dealings with an artist, even when dealing on the phone, in a letter, or through e-mail.

Adapt Your Style to Their Style

This isn't a hypocritical approach. You're just changing style not your personality or core beliefs. If you want to communicate most effectively and most efficiently with different types of people, then you just have to adjust your approach to whatever style will best achieve that goal with that individual's personality. The essential key to success is in knowing your own personality profile. Which type is your type? There are many excellent books on this subject, and I recommend that you study the matter carefully. In the meantime, here's a thumbnail sketch of the basic approaches.

If you're a brain, realize that perfection while a worthy goal is always unattainable. Stop knocking yourself every time you fail to live up to your unrealistic expectations of yourself. You have skills, knowledge, and experience. Stop putting so much emphasis on your weaknesses and focus instead on building on your strengths. When dealing with others, try to be a bit more supportive. Listen more and better and show that you're listening with positive feedback and genuine interest. Come a bit further out of your shell.

If you're a pusher, then please don't push quite so hard. Stop trying to dominate the conversation, the negotiation, and the situation all the time. You can't and you shouldn't try to control the lives, actions, and decisions of other people. Work on developing your people skills. Start listening to what's being said instead of just hearing someone's words. Don't be so stingy with your "good job" or "well done" comments because most other people need more stimulation and motivation than you.

If you're a friend, be a little more aggressive about trying new things. Take a risk now and then even if you have to start small and work your way up to big challenges. Work on becoming a bit more assertive and allow yourself to explore new concepts.

If you're an artist, realize that you're a hardworking and talented real estate professional and that's pretty good. The respect and approval of others is also a good thing, but you can earn genuine respect through real achievement rather than through your efforts to please.

An individual won't be 100 percent of any one personality type. We're all a blend of types, but one always dominates. That's the one you need to discover and to address. Knowing these personalities and responding effectively to them will make a significant difference in the ease and efficiency in reaching your real estate goals. The better you are at working with people, the better you'll be at building your career, fortune, and life.

SECRET OF A MILLIONAIRE REAL ESTATE DEVELOPER

30. Adapt your style to their personality type.

Three Ways We Relate

We humans have thousands of reasons for relating to other humans, but how we relate falls into three basic categories:

1. Visual—what we see
2. Aural—what we hear
3. Tactile—what we touch

In addition to knowing how to adapt your personality type to one of the other four types, you should determine which way the other party in the negotiation relates to other people. That way you can communicate in ways that are most effective according to the way he or she relates to the world. As always, put yourself in the other person's position.

Most people, about six out of ten, relate by what they see. When you hear "I see" or "look here" or some other visually oriented word or phrase, you're probably dealing with a visually oriented person. Your negotiations should include a lot of pictures, visual effects, and word pictures. You can even frame some of your questions visually. Do you see what I mean? Does that paint a picture for you? Am I making things clear?

Don't be automatically offended if someone who relates best by hearing doesn't make a lot of eye contact. He or she is looking away to avoid visual distractions. They're really focusing and trying to hear exactly what you are saying. These folks are working hard at hearing the meaning of your words. "I hear you" or "Listen, I think . . ." are word clues to this type of individual. Be very aware of your words and the meaning of your words when negotiating with these folks. They're picking up everything. Perhaps more than you might realize. So, think before you speak.

People who relate through tactile sensations are "touchy-feely" people who are physically expressive. They're not afraid to hug, kiss, offer a strong handshake, or pat someone on the back. A lot of contact is helpful in negotiations and not all of it has to be person to person. Mock ups, models, brochures, and other physical means of expression can be very useful.

Seven Steps to Winning Any Negotiation

I break any negotiation down into seven basic steps. Some writers have more, some have less, but this breakdown works for me. It helps organize my thinking and my presentation. I think you'll find that they will work pretty well for you. Later on, as you gain experience you can adapt the steps to meet your own style and individual needs. The seven steps are as follows:

1. Make an approach.
2. Listen to gather information.
3. Develop rapport to develop real estate.
4. Make your points.
5. Get agreement along the way.
6. Overcome objections.
7. End successfully.

Let's take a look at each one.

Make an Approach

The initial step in any activity sets the stage for all that follows. I've read from numerous sources that the first meeting you have at the beginning of the business day will shape how you address the challenges and opportunities of that day. A negative encounter can put you in a bad mood, maybe one you don't even recognize. It could spoil your best efforts. That's why I work very hard at starting every day in a great mood and with a positive attitude.

If you have a background in sales, you know something about making an approach to prospects and customers. There are also thousands of books, tapes, CDs, and seminars that address the subject. Some authors have even made such a science out of making an approach that they have pat lines and speeches for virtually every occasion. That's not what I'm talking about. There's a danger to being so letter-perfect in your delivery that you stamp out the essential ingredient of passion.

To me, making an approach is all about attitude. When approaching a negotiation, I want to bring the best possible attitude to the table. I want to be confident. That means I have to prepare my documentation and have to know my presentation backwards and forwards. I want to be upbeat. Knowing the needs of the other party and how my presentation can solve his or her problems gives me that feeling. I want to be positive. That means I focus on getting what I need from the negotiation, not on crushing the other person. If you're confident, upbeat, positive, and if you can show the person you are negotiating with how your proposal solves his or her problem, then you've got the right approach.

Listen to Gather Information

Most of us in this business hear the other party, but only the millionaire real estate developers really listen. There's a big difference, and that makes all the difference in the world. Good listeners have to endure fewer misunderstandings with partners, suppliers, government officials, and clients. They spend fewer hours, less money, and suffer less from headaches, stomach ulcers, and worse conditions from having to clean up the horrible mess caused by a lack of understanding. They raise money easier. Their projects get off the ground faster. They experience fewer hassles and less stress during construction. They close far, far more sales. And it's all because they're a better listener than the next guy.

Listening is an art, and it is one you must develop if you are to conduct successful negotiations. I've seen too many people—many of them quite experienced and talented—blow a negotiation because they rushed in and tried to reach a successful conclusion without really understanding the other party's point of view. The way to win a negotiation is to show how your position, your product or service, and your development, meets the needs of the other person, organization, or group. The only way to do that is to learn those needs, and that requires serious listening.

A good listener will concentrate completely on the other party. He or she watches for body language, such as crossed arms or open palms, that can often communicate true meanings far more eloquently than speech. Like a good reader, a good listener hears "between the lines" and understands the real meaning of what's being said, not just the words and phrases floating on the surface.

Develop Rapport to Develop Real Estate

You don't have to like, admire, or respect someone to be a good negotiator. Some of the most successful negotiations in history have been conducted by bitter enemies after years of strife, mistrust, and even open warfare. What you must have, however, is rapport between the two parties. Rapport is all about finding common ground so that you can communicate as people rather than as titles or positions. Here are four tips to help you find the common ground of rapport:

1. *Pay attention to the other person.* I don't mean offer to go get coffee and donuts. I mean take a look at the individual and his or her office or surroundings. Is she wearing a pin from a service club? Does he have a photo of his family? Is there any indication of a hobby or interest? Are there hints that this person is an athlete who enjoys sports? Does he or she appear angry? Happy? Sad? There are always clues to help you build up a mental picture of the other person.

2. *Ask friendly questions.* I don't mean for you to start an aggressive interrogation, just ask something to get a friendly conversation started. This is where some of the information gleaned from tip number one comes in handy. Your goal isn't to launch into a long discussion about personal matters. You just want enough pleasant chatter to break the

ice. I've completed this step in a matter of a minute or so, but that minute of pleasantness set the tone for the rest of the negotiation.

3. *Take notes.* It's important to get your facts straight. The more important the negotiation, the more important will be the note taking. You don't want to take a transcript of the entire meeting. If that's necessary, tape recorders are inexpensive and readily available. You want notes that are pertinent to getting what you want from the negotiation. I've never run into anyone who objected to me or someone on my staff taking notes. Most often the other party is reassured by my commitment to accuracy.

4. *Listen.* As I indicated in the previous section, listen, and I mean really listen, to what's being said on the other side of the table. Hear the meaning of the words as well as the sound, tone, and inflection of the words.

Make Your Points

I think you'd be amazed at the number of people, many of them experienced professionals, who leave a negotiation only to remember some point or points he or she should have made. "Dang! I meant to say . . ." "I should have told them about . . ." "Why didn't you kick me when I forgot the . . ." A successful negotiation requires that you to make all of your points, generally in a specific order. If you can't remember them all, then bring notes. Rehearsing your presentation is a good way to overcome this hurdle or to at least discover that it's blocking your way.

Get Agreement Along the Way

This is an effective and time-proven sales technique, and it works well in the process of negotiation, too. Your goal is to get the other person to agree with you frequently throughout your presentation. "Yes" doesn't have to be an answer to just serious questions, either. The idea is to get the other person saying yes to a series of questions, simple to serious, leading to that same response to your ultimate and most important question. Used effectively with other techniques, it's a powerful negotiating tool.

Overcome Objections

This is an art in itself. Unfortunately, too many people in a negotiation are terrified of objections. There's just no reason to have that feeling—provided you have the right attitude. An objection, no matter how expressed, is nothing more than someone asking you for a bit more information. That's all. The objection can be angry, disbelieving, or expressing any number of emotions, including timidity, but they're all saying the same thing. "Please, tell me more." Looked at with that frame of mind, you really should be saying "thank you" when you respond with your brilliant and correct answer.

Objections are a natural part of any negotiation. You'll even have some of your own. Some will be serious, and you'll need to have them satisfied before concluding the negotiation. Others will be "gimmes." These are minor objections that you raise, but don't mind letting the other party win. You bring them up and then give them away to provide the other person with a feeling during the process that he or she is winning. Meanwhile, your total focus is on getting exactly what you want at the end of the process.

Be sure when handling objections that you're handling the right one. Listening is key. Repeat the objection back, preferably in the same words, to make doubly sure you got it right. People often bring up one objection, but are actually more concerned about another one. Do whatever digging or exploring is necessary to find the real objection so that you can provide the real answer. Make sure that you have answered the objection to the other party's satisfaction. How do you do that? Ask. If they're not satisfied, keep on providing information until they are satisfied.

End Successfully

A successful end means you've negotiated a conclusion that meets your needs. You may not get 100 percent of what you'd like, but you're satisfied. For example, it would be nice to have your lawyer work for free or for half his or her hourly rate. That's not going to happen. But after you've negotiated a $200 an hour fee down to $175 per hour, you will find yourself very satisfied with your long-term savings.

There's a brutal scene in the film, *The Thomas Crown Affair,* the one with Steve McQueen. A long round of negotiations has been completed. The cigars and champagne are flowing, and the buyers are boasting that they've just acquired a prime "Tommy Crown property." McQueen, cold as ice, looks at the other businessmen and says, "You paid too much." I'd never do that. I might think it, but I'd certainly never say it. Both parties should leave the negotiation satisfied and feeling good about what they've accomplished. And, provided I've gotten what I want out of the negotiation, I don't care if the other person thinks he or she got the better end of the deal. If fact, that's often the mark of the successful end. Everyone is a winner. Really, that's what the art of negotiation is all about.

 SECRET OF A MILLIONAIRE REAL ESTATE DEVELOPER

31. Always employ the seven steps to winning a successful negotiation.

Who Is Running the Show

The most important part of getting anything done is simply recognizing who is the decision maker.

On both sides you have what I call a "system." The system includes a buyer or seller (This party includes not only the person you meet as the property owner, but often his spouse, partner, or group of partners.), respective attorneys, a lender, appraiser, CPA, and others. Identifying the decision maker is key to opening the deal door! As an example, I will often begin discussions with one party and in the initial fact-finding conversation and through further questioning find that really this person needs to involve someone else.

I always ask many questions to discover who's who. My most important questions are: 1) Why are you selling, or buying, now? and 2) Do you have any partners you need to discuss this transaction with, or to whom should I talk? You would be amazed how often you start with the wrong party. The partner is sent out to explore the market, the wife doesn't like managing any more, yet the senior person in the hierarchy does not want to make the deal. Asking such questions is neither time-consuming nor wasted effort. It's an essential task that's guaranteed to speed up and enhance the entire process.

CHAPTER 11

How to Read and
Write a Contract

When a friend deals with a friend, let the bargain be clean and well penn'd, that they may continue friends to the end.

Benjamin Franklin

There's an ancient Arabian saying, "Trust in Allah, but tie your camel." President Reagan echoed that wisdom with his famous warning, "Trust, but verify." Millionaire real estate developers "tie their camels" with the bonds of a contract. From the beginning of your career you should have the services of a good attorney at your disposal. If you do not, you'll have a world of problems on your hands and probably a "world of hurt" to go with them. You're not a lawyer, and you certainly don't understand the complexities of the law and the intricate legal maneuverings that can enhance, entrap, or put an end to a real estate development. A millionaire real estate developer isn't shy about calling in legal counsel, especially when executing a contract.

What Is a Contract?

A contract is an agreement, usually written, between two or more parties in which each becomes in a specified manner obligated to the other. It is a promise or a series of promises recognized by law. Smith agrees to sell Jones his ranch land for $10,000 an acre, the deal to be consummated on January 1, 2005. A contract formalizes the agreement. To be valid, a contract must meet certain standards.

All parties to the contract must be competent. They must be sufficiently mentally alert to realize and understand what they are doing. Someone who is diseased, brain dead, or severely brain damaged, or in some way incapable of making a response is not competent to sign a contract.

The contract must concern itself with a proper subject. A plan to rob a bank may be agreed upon by all parties involved, but the subject is not proper and therefore a contract to do it cannot be legally constructed or consummated.

There must be consideration. One party must pay the other party something. Consideration may be cash, a land swap, or the transfer of ownership of some other valuable item or possibly even a service.

Each party must agree to the contract. There must be mutuality of agreement and of obligation. A contract signed under duress is not enforceable. If you can prove that evil Simon Legree held a gun to your head when you signed over Little Nell's share of the family farm, you are not obligated to accept the terms of that agreement.

You will encounter different types of contracts in your real estate career. For example, oral contracts can be legally enforceable depending on the circumstances. They are very dangerous agreements, and I urge you to work only with written agreements that are approved by your lawyer. Cost-plus contracts require the developer to pay the cost of the project plus a stated percentage of that cost over and above it. That's the contractor's (or other party's) profit. Another type is the bilateral contract in which both parties agree to mutual promises, each becoming the promisor and the promisee. There are other types, but there's no need to launch into a lecture on all the variations available to you. The main point is to have a good lawyer on hand and to make sure he or she is directly involved in developing and executing any contract you sign regardless of type.

Do It Yourself and You Can Do Yourself In

Do not try to write and execute your own contracts. Inasmuch as you lack the knowledge and experience to pull it off, your efforts will surely come back to haunt you. This is why we hire attorneys. A phrase or even a word that you do not fully understand slipped into one of your do-it-yourself contracts could create legal havoc during the project. Worse than shooting your-self in the foot, you could be creating financial suicide.

If you want to take a hands-on approach to contract writing, okay. Draft your basic document, *but then give it to your attorney for review, revision, and writing.* This is a must. You'll probably be amazed at some of the financial or legal corners you've unwittingly written yourself into. Show the professional what you want and then let him or her put it into the proper words and phrases.

I've seen standard real estate contract forms offered at bookstores. Some of those contract templates may be useful to you as a base document, but every negotiation and every contract is unique. The usefulness of a prefab contract can only take you so far. If you go this route, make any modifications you think necessary, *but then give it to your attorney for review, revision, and writing.* It doesn't matter how well written that store-bought document may be, it wasn't written for you and your specific real estate development. Aristotle said there's a foolish corner in the brain of every wise person. A wise real estate developer knows that, refuses to paint himself or herself into that corner, and calls in a professional to handle a professional's job.

Basic Elements of a Contract

As I said, every contract is unique. Still, there are elements that are com-mon to all or at least to most. You don't have to be a lawyer to be a million-aire real estate developer, but you must have a fundamental understanding of the basics. Every contract will have certain essential elements.

Names, Addresses, and Phone Numbers

The seller's name usually appears first in the contract, followed by his or her address and phone number. A specific address for the property being sold is listed next.

Amount of the Down Payment

This is a specific figure and is either an agreed-upon dollar amount or a percentage of the purchase price. In those rare cases in which there is no down payment, this clause would obviously not be necessary. A down payment is sometimes called earnest money because it shows that you are a serious, therefore, an earnest, buyer.

Terms of the Mortgage and Financing

A buyer needs a mortgage to buy the property, and this section describes the terms of that mortgage. Generally speaking, a 100 percent mortgage is not possible or at best is a very rare opportunity. For instance, the typical purchase of a house calls for an 80 percent mortgage with a 20 percent down payment. The contract will state these or whatever terms are agreed upon. This section notes the

- amount mortgaged,
- buyer's interest rate,
- amortization schedule,
- balloon note period, if any, and
- time period allocated for payback of the mortgage loan to the lender.

This section of the contract may also contain a number of other features or stipulations depending on the negotiations prior to drawing up the agreement.

Date of Possession

There must be an official and legal point in time by which the buyer takes possession of the property from the seller. This moment must be specified in the contract. Usually, possession occurs when the deed has been transferred and the seller has received his or her money for the property.

In some cases, you may have some flexibility, and it may be possible to negotiate possession prior to the closing of the sale. In other cases, the seller may require additional time to vacate the property, and the date of possession may actually occur at some point after the buyer becomes the new owner. This is called an "owner use and occupancy" clause. Many items in a contract are negotiable. For example, as the buyer/developer you may willingly agree to allow the owner a short period of time, say 30 days past closing, in which to move out. If additional days are required, you may insert a clause noting that you will be paid a specified daily rent until the property is vacated.

The goal isn't to win for the sake of winning, to beat someone down, or to take advantage of any one or any situation. You want a smooth transition from seller to buyer so that you can go about enhancing your millionaire status. It's in everyone's interest to be flexible and work, as much as possible, with the other party to ensure that transition. A sound contract covering all the bases is one of the best means possible of achieving that goal.

Attorney Approval Clause

An attorney approval clause is an essential clause and necessary for your protection. This little paragraph makes sure that your attorney has enough time to thoroughly review the contract and make any comments, recommendations, or revisions prior to its execution. If the seller becomes pushy and resists the inclusion of an attorney approval clause, something is probably wrong with the property or the deal. I hate to sound like attorney Johnny Cochran, but if the seller balks, take a walk.

Inspection Period

If the seller balks at allowing sufficient time for you to inspect the property you're considering purchasing, there's probably something rotten in Denmark. Or the floorboards. Or the roof joists. Or with the seller. Certainly you have given any property you're considering a thorough walk-through. A professional inspector that you have hired should at some time before the sale follow in your footsteps. He or she will see things you'd never notice. Some of those things might be enough to cause you to back out of the deal, such as those rotten floorboards. Other inspections might reveal treasures not even known by the current owner, such as beautiful hardwood floors hidden beneath the old carpet. The point is that you have to know exactly what you're buying, and you must be allowed sufficient time to do that.

Closing Date

This clause specifies the date that the seller hands over the deed to the property and the buyer reciprocates by handing over his or her check for that property. This is the day when the buyer becomes the owner.

Boilerplate and Why It Is Essential

Boilerplate refers to contract clauses or items so standardized that they are included automatically in all contracts. Like the steel plates used to make boilers, these elements are slapped together to form the shell of a basic contract. They are so commonly used that the attorneys for both sides usually have no qualms about their inclusion. Boilerplate is essential because it covers matters that generally shouldn't have to be negotiated with every contract. The proper use of boilerplate saves hours of time for buyer and seller and a significant amount of money that would otherwise be eaten up in unnecessary legal fees.

Still, make sure your attorney carefully reviews with you all boilerplate in any contract. Much or all of it may be in legal terms that you do not understand. If that's the situation, get your lawyer to explain the items to you in plain English. It's easy to slip a phrase or sentence more favorable to one party than the other into boilerplate. This is especially true if an attorney thinks the other doesn't read the material carefully "because it's, you know, just boilerplate."

Legal terminology drives me crazy. "Why can't they just say what they mean in plain English!" The lack of complete understanding is frustrating, as is paying my attorney to explain it to me as if I were a kid in kindergarten. Well, in a way I am in kindergarten and so are you. But I recognize the need for highly specific and technical language and the need for professionals who can communicate and conduct business using it.

Our legal system is extremely complex and getting more so all the time. As that process continues, there's a need for specific, legally definable terms and phrases. There's even a need for jargon. Don't feel too bad or intimidated. Every profession has its own special "lingo." Your attorney would feel just as lost if he were to accompany you on a job site and listen in on a conversation between you and a contractor. "Yeah, the design calls for a cornice with lentils under the second story balustrade right near the quoins." The point is that without that language our contracts and agreements would be much less specific. There'd be a lot more room for "interpretation" of the agreement by the involved parties. When you get two or more parties interpreting the meaning of a single fact, you often end up with a fight on your hands. Legal language takes out much if not all of the costly and time-consuming legal wrangling in a contract and is therefore worth the hassle. Remember that ambiguity, even if you think you know what the clause refers to, may do considerable harm to your interests. If a judge doesn't clearly understand it, he or she will probably assume that that the other party can't figure it out either. If you created the ambiguity, the ruling could easily go against you.

An old Spanish proverb says to sign nothing without reading it. That's true, but I'd add a caveat. Sign nothing without understanding it.

Elements You Want to Include in Your Contract

You'll probably remember from Chapter 6 the four elements I believe should be in every construction contract: the developer's right to terminate the relationship with the contractor provided his subcontractors do not meet the specifications or deadlines of the project; the developer's right to remove a lien placed on your property; a firm completion date and even project-specific deadlines within that time frame; your protection from the use of substandard materials or workmanship by the contractor or subcontractors.

Elements that you will want to include in other contracts are

- penalties upon the contractor for delays and the cost of the damage due from the delay; and
- guarantees and warrantees; i.e., adequate insurance coverage naming you and your lender as additional insured party/parties.

Your attorney will have specifics based on his or her experience and in accordance to the rules and regulations of the individual state and region involved.

Elements You Want to Exclude from Your Contract

Contracts are all about negotiation, and you'll be negotiating with some real sharpies throughout your career. They'll try to end-run all kinds of articles and clauses immensely favorable to their position. Even when dealing with a person or company that is on the up and up, you can't blame the other side for trying to make the best deal possible. There are a number of items that you'll see in print, sometimes very fine print, you'll definitely want excluded from your contracts. Here are a few of the major problems from my point of view.

Always have a short cure period on behalf of your opposing party. To cure means to fix or settle the item. You need a long cure time, and they should have a short cure time.

Never accept responsibility to do construction on interiors for commercial tenants. You will be burdened with damages from the delays accompanied by the construction, and the tenant will seek damages. You only control the space, not the construction. Let the tenant do the construction of their space. And let them spend the money as well. They will often experience cost overruns. Cost overruns should not be your burden.

When Can You Break a Contract?

You never make an agreement planning to break it, but sometimes that act becomes necessary. It's best to negotiate a favorable conclusion to any disagreement, but we all know that's not always possible. If the other party just isn't living up to the agreement and you can't find a reasonable solution, then it's time to "do what ya gotta do." Remember that your money will not become refundable, called "hard," until four contract stipulations are met. These are:

1. The attorney approval period
2. The inspection period
3. An environmental audit
4. The mortgage contingency

Once you've allowed these deadlines to pass without raising an objection, the deal is officially moving on. It's important to be on your toes every step of the way.

There are two potential areas in the contract that might give you the opportunity to break it. The first is the attorney approval period. If there's something wrong with the agreement, your attorney can scream "halt" and put a screaming end to your misery. The inspection period offers another opportunity. If the property isn't as described, then you can probably break the contract with little or no trouble. For example, if the contract describes a "wetland," but the wet turns out to be creosote leaked from the nearby telephone pole factory, clearly that property has been misrepresented.

Of course, if the seller does not live up to his or her promises in the contract, you have cause for breaking it. This doesn't mean everything will work out to your complete satisfaction. For one thing, a deal you've been planning on has fallen through. All your plans will have to be adjusted accordingly, and that can be an expensive proposition. Secondly, regardless of the reason behind your move, you're the one actually breaking the contract. Legally the seller may be entitled to keep the down payment. The seller may even try to squeeze you for damages, but if you've structured your contract properly that won't happen.

Inevitably, you'll be rolling along on some great real estate development deal and out of the blue the seller will want to break the contract. Fortunately for us developers, the law puts a greater burden of proof on the seller in the breaking of a contract. In signing, the seller commits himself to the legal "specific performance" of that contract. That means he or she has to honor his agreement to deliver the property you want to buy at the agreed upon price and at the agreed upon time.

"The property you want" from the previous sentence is an important consideration. Every piece of property is unique. As a developer, you've developed your plans, construction schedules and teams, budgets, timetables, and end use around that specific property. You can never ever find another one exactly like it on the face of the earth. Backing out of the deal automatically puts you in a terrible bind. It's a bind recognized by the courts.

SECRET OF A MILLIONAIRE REAL ESTATE DEVELOPER

32. No matter what excuse is offered, there's always only one reason sellers want to break a contract. They think they can get a better deal somewhere else.

Let's say you've entered into an agreement to purchase some property near Orlando. Everything is rolling along fine until the seller hears a rumor that Disney is expanding. Whoa! Because Disney has far deeper pockets than you or me, the seller gets greedy and wants to break the agreement. The ethical thing to do is buy out your contract, but that doesn't always happen. Again, that's why we hire good lawyers.

I operate my business according to the philosophy that my word is my bond. Believe me, your reputation precedes you and hangs around long after you have left the meeting, building, or community. While writing this book, one of the salespeople in my real estate office was representing a condominium buyer. The agent brought her to a building that appeared to be perfect for all her needs. She liked a unit, wrote a contract with my salesperson, and the offer was submitted to the developer, someone I had known for more than ten years.

This developer worked on the greater fool theory—no matter how bad you treat your customers today, there's always a greater fool to victimize just around the corner. His reputation was so poor in Chicago that many Realtors boycotted his projects. They did so because through the years this man had dedicated himself to building a bad reputation. He is not dependable, his warrantees are worthless, and because he makes a new buyer suffer, his performance is a poor reflection on all developers. My salesperson is new to the business and did not know that this developer's reputation was a terrible one. Good Realtors may do business with this guy once, but after the experience they'll never return. He just creates too much grief for all concerned. When I was following up on the progress of the contract presentation and the conclusion of the deal, I found that it was never ending. Not only was it not moving to a finial negotiation, but the developer kept reneging on terms of the contract. He was upsetting the buyer by taking back his word, guarantees, and promises.

Remember, everyone wants to win, and that is the success of the deal. The buyer was not only getting nothing, but was experiencing losses and getting agreed-upon items taken away. When I found out the name of seller/developer, I suggested, for the good of the client, that the agent join the many who boycott this guy's developments because the developer was so undependable. My suggestion was taken seriously, and the buyer bought elsewhere. Remember, your reputation precedes you, most of the time. Bad news travels fast, and it will always catch up with you.

Remember, the courts serve the function of resolving the disputes of written contracts!

 SECRET OF A MILLIONAIRE REAL ESTATE DEVELOPER

33. Always keep your word.

Victor Kiam, President of Norelco, did a marvelous job of expressing that philosophy when he said, "Your handshake is your bond. As far as I'm concerned, a handshake is worth more than a signed contract. As an entrepreneur, a reputation for integrity is your most valuable commodity. If you try to put something over on someone, it will come back to haunt you." Trust. Verify. And always keep your word.

I'd like to wrap up by reminding you that a good contract must be "well penn'd," and that means well-considered, carefully thought through, and reviewed by your attorney. I believe in "well penn'd" contracts backed by the unshakeable word of honest parties.

Taxes

The Eiffel Tower is the Empire State Building after taxes.

Anonymous

People in the real estate business pay a lot of taxes, and there's no use complaining about the annual check or those numbers at the bottom of a sales slip. Taxes are eternal. The good news is that you don't have to allow taxation to pick your bones clean. Your Empire State Building of a business doesn't have to end up looking like the empty framework that is the Eiffel Tower.

Taxes are essential in modern society. FDR reminded folks that taxes are the price of living in an organized society. Although sometimes I think we're a bit "overorganized," that's how we pay for our schools, roads, parks, and a list of services that is the envy of the rest of the world. If you own property and buy and sell property, the government requires that you pay for the privilege. All governments—local, state, and federal—have their hands out reaching for their share of your dollars. As your real estate career advances, you will pay more and more taxes. It's part of the cost of doing business. But it's also part of your job to make sure that those taxes don't do you in. That's a twofold process: (1) paying your fair share and no more, and (2) avoiding problems with the IRS. Both chores can be tricky prospects even for the most honest businesspeople working with the best of intentions.

Capital Gains and Ordinary Income

Get to know these terms and all their implications because these are the two primary ways you'll pay your real estate taxes. Every time there's an upcoming election, we hear a lot about raising, lowering, or eliminating capital gains taxes. We'll see, but in the meantime realize that capital gains are nothing more than the profits you make from selling real estate. Here's an example. Let's say that in year 2000 you bought 40 acres of raw land for $100,000. According to the IRS, you must own that land for a year to fall into the category of capital gains taxation. Time passes, and in 2005 the nearby city has moved five miles closer and that land is now worth $150,000. You sell and pocket a nice $50,000 profit. That $50,000 is your capital gain, and Uncle Sam will want to get his share. If the city had moved the other way and the value of your land dropped to, say $85,000, your $15,000 loss would be reported as a capital loss on your income tax.

Ordinary income includes salaries, fees, commissions, interest, dividends, and other means of producing income. As it applies to real estate, it's an inventory tax. Our inventory just happens to be property rather than blue jeans, automobile parts, soap, soup, or sugar. Currently ordinary income is taxed at twice the rate of capital gains. When selling property, it's frequently in your best interest to do so in the window of opportunity for capital gains.

If you use the property you've purchased for rental income, that tenant income is considered ordinary income. As a landlord you'll maintain and repair that property. If you plan to sell it, you'll probably make a few extra efforts to make the property extra attractive. Those costs are considered expenses by the IRS and are not taxed.

Here's a simple way to look at the difference between the two methods of taxation. Ordinary income is income earned through ordinary means, such

---

SECRET OF A MILLIONAIRE REAL ESTATE DEVELOPER

34. Always have a qualified financial professional keep an eye on the ever-changing local, state, and federal tax laws, rules, and regulations.

as the sale of your inventory of properties. Capital gains refers to taxes paid on that property after it has been held for an extended period of time.

A warning: the tax code and tax laws change about as fast as the weather. Between the time I write this book and its publication, something somewhere will surely have changed, perhaps radically so. Please, always consult with your tax advisor and accountant on all matters relating to taxation.

Local Taxes

There's an old saying that all politics is local. That's not quite true about taxation. Still, although you are privileged to pay taxes on the state and federal levels, most of the taxes you pay will be to local authorities. These taxes fall into two categories: visible taxes and hidden taxes. The following is a very brief introduction into the most likely versions of each you'll encounter. Again, always consult with your accountant and financial advisor before adopting any tax policies. Laws, codes, restrictions, rules, and regulations vary from state to state and from community to community. Listen to the advice of millionaire real estate developers from all across the land: when it comes to paying your taxes, *double-check everything before you do anything.* I'd be willing to bet a good steak at a great steakhouse that your community will at least levy the following taxes on real estate.

Visible Taxes

A *transfer tax* is charged whenever property moves from one owner to another, and it's most likely the single largest real estate tax in your community. In other words, it's a fee your municipality charges for the right to conduct business within its boundaries. The concept is basic. If you're making money here, if you're using our roads, bridges, utilities, and services to earn your living, you should carry your fair share of the load.

Here in Chicago, I'm charged $7.50 for every $1,000 in value of a property I sell. Sometimes that hurts, but it's hard to argue the logic of the tax law. We real estate folks do drive on the streets, turn on the electricity, drink the water, and enjoy the fact that our garbage disappears every week. Those are some of the benefits that attract the nice people who write the nice checks that purchase our properties.

Property within a city is usually subject to a *registration fee*, a flat fee that as this book is being written probably runs $50 or less per property. You pay a price for having something that exists. I think this one evolved from the municipal philosophy of "If it's out there, tax it!"

A *signage fee* is charged, obviously, against your sign or in some cases all of your signs, even those within or on the same property.

In addition to taxing individual buildings and even signs within a building, some municipalities even tax components of a building. A *boiler inspection fee* or some such similar tax may be assessed.

A *building permit fee* is a tax on making things better. If you make improvements to your property or if you engage in new construction, you'll probably pay a percentage of your investment in those improvements to the municipality.

You may face *parking* taxes or fees if your property has a parking lot, parking garage, or parking spaces. There's no telling what else is taxed in your area. Rest assured that if it exists, whatever it may be, someone somewhere is working on a plan to write you a tax bill for it.

Every city is different. Every city taxes real estate and real estate developers. Every city is looking for more ways to tax more people, places, and things. That's another reason to find and work closely with a top accountant and financial advisor. Millionaire real estate developers always pay their fair share. We also know that local, state, and federal taxation is a swamp that must be traversed. We get the best guides possible to get us through with the least amount of lost baggage along the way.

Hidden Taxes

Whenever you hear a politician asking you to "make an investment" in the city, state, or nation, you have to know that he or she is really saying, "I want to raise your taxes." They're not fooling anyone, at least not in the business community. Hidden taxes, fees, and costs that are called something other than what they really are can be found everywhere. For example, Washington politicians are wary of the "T-word" these days and have been using the word "investment" instead. Regardless of what you call it, a tax is still a tax. These costs may not represent a direct exchange of money from citizen to government. Often they're tasks the property owner must do at his or her own expense according to the dictates of the municipality. Call it "civic improvements" or whatever you want. The process has a government requisitioning your money for its own purposes and that to me that is still a tax.

Height restrictions, sometimes called "down-zoning" or "overlay districts," are put in place to reduce the size of the residential population, improve the quality of life for the citizenry, and so on. That may be true, but in effect it's also a major tax. If a developer has to stop developing a property at an arbitrary height, that height limit also is a limit on income. Reduced income at the direction of a municipality is in effect a tax. What happens when you can develop only 16 instead of 20 units on a property? One, your expenses remain about the same. Two, your income is reduced. Three, you have to raise the rent on your tenants to make up the difference. Four, once again the consumer is forced by the government "protecting" him or her to make up the difference.

Some cities have a *green fee.* Chicago has one, and it's nothing more than a tax despite the pleasant-sounding title. If I develop a building with 12 or more units, I'm charged a $2,500 green fee that is applied to making improvements in the city's parks and green spaces. I'm all for parks and recreation. They improve the quality of life and attract more people and investors into the community. But the parks are shared by all. Why do the cities single out real estate developers for a special tax? The answer is simple. Because they can, that's why.

Chicago has a few other ways of squeezing city services out of its developers. When I build a new town house, I'm required by the city to place a decorative iron fence between the building and the streets. Developers are also mandated by the city to place green spaces outside such new properties. Unfortunately, this isn't really a tax on the developers. Why? Because, as with all businesses, taxes are passed along to the consumer in the purchase price. Again, John Q. Public takes it in the shorts, not because of the developers, but due to the actions of the city. Check around your area before investing in a real estate development. Hidden taxes may not, and probably should not, discourage you from continuing with your plans. However, you should know all your likely costs before you proceed, including all the hidden taxes your friendly neighborhood politicians have mandated.

State Taxes

The bulk of your real estate taxes will be handed over to your local government, but your state will have its hand out, too. As with all taxing bodies, the act is a play on the old "carrot and stick" management technique. Only in this situation you have the carrot, they want it, and they have the stick to make sure you fork it over.

You'll probably pay your state taxes yearly and in the form of taxes on revenue and on the transfer of property. You may also be required to pay certain licensing fees. Again, these rules and regulations change as often as the politicians can change them. Stay in close contact with your accountant and tax advisor, especially as tax time rolls around.

Federal Taxes

I believe Laurence J. Peter, author of *The Peter Principle,* wrote that we actually live under two forms of government: the long form and the short form. He's right. One way or another, the federal government will get its hands on some of your real estate (and other) earnings. Federal taxes on real estate developers are revenue taxes. How much or what percentage depends on your corporate structure. Generally, you face two roads regarding your revenue and the resulting tax liabilities. One, you can take all or part of that money out of the corporation or partnership as income. Naturally, you'll be taxed on it. Two, you can reinvest all or part of it back into the company or in other real estate ventures.

There's no right or wrong, better or worse scenario that applies across the board. What's best for you depends on you, your business, your current assets and liabilities, your plans for the future, and so on. A good accountant and tax advisor is essential if you're to find the safest, surest way through the federal taxation swamp.

Working with the "Taxman"

Here are a few general tax guidelines I've developed over the years. Consider them in light of your own situation and use, adapt, or ignore them to your best advantage as you see fit.

Hire the best accountant and financial advisor you can. This is not an area in which to trim the budget. Every dollar you "save" by using a less-talented,

---

☞ **SECRET OF A MILLIONAIRE REAL ESTATE DEVELOPER**

35. Work with the local, state, and federal "taxman" rather than against him.

---

less-experienced, or less-dedicated advisor can multiply voraciously and come back in the form of additional payments, penalties, or even time behind bars.

Accept responsibility for your actions. Invest time with your accountant to discuss all aspects of your tax return before you file it. If you have questions, get answers and make sure they're satisfactory answers. The bottom line is and will remain that it's your name and signature on the tax form. It's your responsibility to make sure that the form is correct in every detail. If you shirk that responsibility, well, it's also your tush in the proverbial sling.

Don't even think of evading payment. They may be an inefficient bureaucracy. They may not be able to explain their own tax code. They may be the butt of the latest joke from Leno or Letterman, but when it comes to catching tax cheats, you'd be amazed at the tireless, eternal pursuit that can be mounted by the IRS. Remember, there's no statute of limitations on tax fraud. As I said, *eternal.*

Outside of the fact that tax evasion crosses legal and moral lines, it's also expensive. Let's say your accountant slipped up and made a genuine mistake in your forms. Things happen, and the IRS understands. Of course, there's a matter of a 5 percent penalty for any amount unpaid, but that's the price of doing business. You write the check, say you're sorry, kick yourself, and move on. Change the scenario so that you used fraudulent documents to evade paying your taxes and that penalty jumps to 50 percent. If paying 5 percent hurts, paying 50 percent is downright torture. And you'd be bringing it on yourself. Additionally, you could also risk jail time. The risk is never worth the gamble.

Don't argue with the "taxman." You'd be playing with a stacked deck, and the other guy would be holding all the good cards. For example, let's say you've been taking a deduction for years, but all of a sudden that deduction is disallowed. There's no use fighting the decision. Because you're playing with their deck on their table, you can only make things worse by popping off. How? Well, if you get the IRS agent riled up enough, he or she might just decide that all those allowed deductions for all those years should be disallowed. Suddenly, you owe a lot of back taxes.

Yes, they can do that.

Don't freak out if you're audited. An audit is nothing more than a procedure. It's not an accusation of anything nor should any stigma be attached to it. Thousands of people undergo the process every year. Upon being notified, just keep cool. Contact your accountant and your lawyer for instructions. Get all your paperwork organized and refamiliarize yourself with the materials.

It's very unlikely that you're being singled out because of that vote for Ross Perot back in the 1980s. There's probably a minor error that needs correcting or a basic question that needs a simple answer. You'll be notified via the mail and will be told what you need to do, where you need to go, and what you need to bring. One of the things I recommend you bring is a positive attitude. Don't turn a simple procedure into an adversarial situation. Again, "they got ya outnumbered, fella."

There's no reason to feel guilty. So, don't bring in a lot of records and data to "prove" your innocence. There's no use opening financial doors that can remain closed. Just bring what is requested and no more.

If you're really nervous about going through an audit, then don't. You do that by making sure that your tax forms are 100 percent correct before you send them in. As with most situations in real estate, a little work and preparation on the front end eliminates a lot of problems on the back end.

Tax Benefits Associated with Real Estate

Taxation is considered such a negative subject and is such an unpopular topic across the board that I wanted to end this chapter on a positive note. And there are positive notes, even when it comes to taxes. A lot of expenses directly associated with real estate development can be written off on your tax forms. These expenses may include supplies for maintenance and repair of your property, personnel wages, property taxes, interest on borrowed capital, leasing commissions, insurance premiums, and perhaps other expenses.

Certain noncash charges may be deductible, such as depreciation on capital costs and improvements on your property or properties. Investment tax credits on income-creating tangible property may also apply. Property tax abatements may also be applicable to historic properties, real estate in neighborhoods on the decline, and even to other types of properties. Naturally, you'll have to jump through bureaucratic hoops, fill out the appropriate forms, and make sure that your properties fully comply with all the rules and regulations.

As always, check closely with your accountant and tax advisor to see exactly what rules, regulations, laws, benefits, and restrictions apply to you and to your properties. Or, have I said that before?

CHAPTER 13

Government Relations: Working with Local, State, and Federal Governments

Government today sits as an invisible partner of every company, every family, and every individual in the country.

William L. Wearly

Regardless of where you are considering developing property, you are going to find different zoning and municipal codes that will dictate, in every sense of the word, what you can and can't build. There's no place in the nation where you will not be required to deal with government bureaucracies. I agree with Mr. Wearly that government is a partner, but I take issue with his use of "invisible." Governments are quite easy to spot, actually. You can't miss 'em. In fact, you aren't permitted to miss 'em. And if you try, there are often severe penalties for making the effort.

 SECRET OF A MILLIONAIRE REAL ESTATE DEVELOPER

36. Play according to the rules or you'll lose the game.

Politics always plays a role in everything. In the City of Chicago (and often in your area as well), before attempting anything, be sure to inform your local alderman or city councilman. Certainly you must work closely with the alderman to change zoning, change the use of an existing property, or do something unusual, but you need to have the alderman on your side, too.

Remember the story I told in Chapter 1. If only I had waited until the elections for aldermen had been concluded, I would have saved myself and/or made myself a lot of money. It's true! Make your project known and disclose it to the alderman while it's on the drawing board.

There is a rule in Chicago that you cannot get a building permit without an "alley access letter." This document is actually a letter of permission from the alderman stating that you can use the alley running behind the property for access for deliveries and so on. This letter is a safeguard for the alderman. It provides an alert that a real estate transaction is going on in his or her domain. Without this letter, you can't get a building permit in Chicago.

Here's another example. You will encounter tight restrictions for area ratio requirements on your construction projects. If you fail to comply, you'll also encounter a "stop work order" from a local governing body. Then you'll get to enjoy watching "your tax dollars at work" grinding your development, and perhaps your business, to a standstill. If you violate too many rules and regulations, you could face consequences far worse than inconvenience or financial penalties.

The rules will change from neighborhood to neighborhood, city to city, and state to state. Building requirements usually begin at a local level where communities will dictate what they will and will not allow to be built within their jurisdictions. These laws change with each generation and each development boom. Government bureaucrats, regulators, and politicians just love to govern. During the past ten years, Chicago has instituted a height restriction ordinance, a town home ordinance, overlay districts in respective areas of the city, down-zoning, as well as a complete rewrite of the zoning codes, which were last rewritten in 1956. The City of Chicago has certainly changed in the years 1956 through 2004 as has every city in the world. Often there is a legitimate need for change. Codes that were acceptable 11 years after the end of World War II have changed as building materials and technologies have changed, as populations and population demands have changed, and as our lifestyles have changed.

Try to imagine a world without fast-food restaurants, strip shopping centers, and the numbers of condominiums and town houses we now see. Changes in the way we live, work, and enjoy life have by necessity brought about changes in real estate development regulation. Parts of many cities considered blighted inner-city areas in the 1950s are now filled with loft buildings that are homes as well as art galleries and offices. There have been significant changes, and change is a constant factor in real estate development. Expect more.

It's important to understand that although a piece of property may have been in a location for years or even decades, it may not at present comply with all the new rules, regulations, and standards. If your objective is to renovate the property, be sure that you are aware of any new laws that you will need to comply with in order to use the existing property. Don't assume and don't take the word of another party. Check it out yourself.

In a meeting I attended while writing this book, I was approached by a Realtor who told me of a mixed-use building. It was vacant, he said, and prime for redevelopment in an area of Chicago near White Sox Baseball Park, a highly desirable area for a developer looking for a good deal. The physical appearance of the building was attractive, and I believed it would be a good development opportunity for retail stores and apartments. The Realtor warned me that the zoning for the retail portion was restrictive and began to list businesses that were prohibited from using this space. The community had kept the zoning restrictive to avoid gentrification. They didn't want a Starbucks on every corner in their neighborhood nor did they want a McDonald's, Subway, Gap, or any of the retailers that we see in communities from coast to coast. The objective was to keep this community a community of mom-and-pop neighborhood businesses.

At this moment I don't know if I will be interested in this property because of the difficulties that I may have in attempting to rezone the real estate. It would be an uphill battle with this community. They have the right to attempt to maintain the status quo just as I have a right to make the attempt to change it. Whenever evaluating property, remember all is not what it appears to be. When researching properties, you naturally create a fantasy image of what you can build. Before you can try to make that fantasy a reality, you have to look at the zoning laws and understand how they impact your development economically. Fantasize all you want, but at some point apply a heavy dose of common sense. Some fantasies just aren't meant to be.

Here's an example of how regulation can impact town home developers. This happened in the Chicago market where height restriction ordinances were implemented in 1998 and 2000. The higher a property could be built, the more value the land had because a taller building allowing two-level units and better views could demand a higher price. The new town home ordinance restricted the amount of land that the town home could occupy by requiring that the developer provide green space for each development. For example, although a yard would be very small as square footage standards go, the developer would have to provide that space by cutting back the living space in the unit itself. This meant a piece of land that might support the construction of six units could only have five. That's one-sixth of the developer's potential profit down the drain before the project could even get off the ground. You need to acquire that type of information in your initial evaluation or due diligence of the property. Include the regulated restrictions in your lender package noting what you can build and how you are going to build it.

Often it's wise to schedule a meeting with the councilman or alderman to determine the current zoning restrictions on the piece of property you're considering. Take time to inquire about any possible zoning changes that are on the drawing board or are being considered for future implementation, too. It's important to recognize early on that the local alderman or councilman is the person who will have to support your zoning change for a piece of property should you require a change in the use or the setback requirements and modifications for your ratio of building to land. The alderman will also know with whom you may need to meet from the local neighborhood and community councils from which you will need to gain support.

There is certainly a cost involved in rezoning a property, and many developers feel that they are best suited and can operate efficiently when dealing with "as of rights of zoning." *As of rights zoning* means not attempting to change anything in building that your rights allow you to build based on the current zoning of the property. Be aware that different cities and municipalities have watchdogs even for "as of rights zoning." The "alley access letter" mentioned earlier is a good example. The document is important because Chicago has lots of alleys that get a lot of use by the public and especially the business community. In building and renovating property, many trucks and delivery vehicles will be accessing the property through the alleys. The alley access letter has to be maintained to avoid citations for deliveries and for parking in garages that may have alley access only. The city fathers take a dim view of tying up traffic, restricting commercial access, and inconveniencing the citizenry. They take an even dimmer view of developers who ignore the rules of their game.

If you are going to be an active developer, purchasing a zoning book from your local municipality is a good idea. Zoning laws may be modified from year to year, and supplements should be made available. You should keep up to speed, but it is unlikely that the entire zoning code will be rewritten more than once every generation. Having the zoning codes for your city for quick referral in your office will prove to be an invaluable convenience and well worth whatever price the city will charge.

Dealing with the Bureaucratic Mentality

The difference between a business mentality and a bureaucratic mentality is simply this: in business we try to do things quickly. Time is money, and enthusiasm drives our projects. Bureaucrats have nothing but time on their hands and have no sense of urgency at all. They are very happy maintaining the status quo and avoiding conflicts or confrontations. You rarely see a bureaucrat stick his or her neck out for a project. Generally they try to avoid or skirt an issue. But business still has to be done, and as a developer you are one of the people who have to do it. Once the bureaucracy gets involved in your project, things will slow down. It's important to factor in such slowdowns in the time frame and financing of your project.

This book is filled with many references to the work that we have done in Chicago because that is where I live, but the lessons will apply to every community even though the technical specifics may not. For example, the bureaucratic machine in Chicago's Department of Buildings in the late 1990s had virtually ground to a halt. Back in the early 1990s, a building permit could be obtained within a matter of six to eight weeks, but a decade later the time required to obtain a permit dealing with a bureaucratic trade inspectors down in City Hall was a nightmare. The harder one might push, the slower things became. And it didn't matter who you knew or what you knew. Everything went slowly. The computerization of the Department of Buildings as well as the frequent change of the commissioner of buildings created obstacles in every way, shape, and form for those who were in the building business. Nothing changed until John Roberson was appointed Building Commissioner in 2001 by Mayor Daley. He took the approach that construction should be profitable, and he literally redesigned how the Department of Buildings worked. That is, the department worked when the developers worked.

What I mean here is really quite simple. In a bureaucracy, especially when it comes to obtaining building permits, it is important that your presentation is letter-perfect. I am not exaggerating a bit. That means every drawing has to be perfect. There can be no ambiguities in the text, nothing left out of the data, and all facts and figures must be accurate and up to date. There

SECRET OF A MILLIONAIRE REAL ESTATE DEVELOPER

37. Work closely with your architect.

can be no room for question, and it must be free of errors because questions and errors will delay the project.

Inaccurate or incomplete drawings may need to be sent back for corrections. Ambiguities have to be answered, and this ping-pong method of submission and rejection, submission and rejection, will delay your project and cost you more time and money and create more frustration than you ever believed possible. I had Mr. Roberson speak to the Chicago Association of Realtors Spring 2002 Convention. What he said in his opening remarks was striking. "Government is good at raising taxes and implementing wars; none of these things are productive items. They are always viewed as unproductive."

That's a good point about how bureaucracy functions. But we who depend upon the bureaucracy have to haul our share of the regulatory load, too. Mr. Roberson also pointed out in defense of Chicago's Department of Buildings that many unnecessary delays occurred because architects presented incomplete project plans. When building inspectors in the building department reviewed the respective drawings for permits, they had to stop when projects were not complete on paper and important questions remained unanswered. A light went on. It occurred to me that that was exactly what I had experienced in two matters that delayed permits for me and that is why I bring it up to you. Again, the specifics may vary from community to community, but the lesson applies everywhere.

SECRET OF A MILLIONAIRE REAL ESTATE DEVELOPER

38. Always make your projections as letter-perfect, as complete, and as up to date as humanly possible.

This book is a learning tool. Study and learn from my experience so that when you deal with government bureaucrats you will make sure that your architects have shown you and allowed you to understand everything in every drawing that has been put together for the project. If you, the developer, can't understand it, then someone who isn't very sophisticated in the real world marketplace can't understand it. As a new person in this business, you need to know how and why things get done. The sooner you grasp that, the sooner your career will start blossoming.

If you are reading this book, you have a certain level of intelligence and interest in professional real estate development. Always do your best to work *with* not *against* the bureaucracy so that you can put those skills to work building developments instead of fighting city hall.

CHAPTER 14

Insurance

Insurance, n. An ingenious modern game of chance in which the player is permitted to enjoy the comfortable conviction that he is beating the man who keeps the table.

Ambrose Bierce, *The Devil's Dictionary*

You can't be a millionaire real estate developer without superior insurance. The reason is basic. Without insurance someone will take those millions away from you. Because insurance coverage is a critical need, the subject deserves your undivided attention. Your business (and you) will need different types of insurance, and those needs will probably change somewhat throughout your career. Developers on the Gulf Coast don't have a lot of worries about earthquakes, but the smart ones surely have protection against hurricane damage. There's an old joke that developers in California only have to insure against four things: earth, wind, fire, and water. You'd think developers in Arizona's deserts wouldn't need flood insurance, but every once in a while the rains do come. Those dry river beds get wet and create havoc when the flood waters come roaring out of their banks. And those smoldering volcanoes in Washington have been quiet lately, but . . .

Every developer's needs are unique. It's hard to make recommendations across the board, but I'll make a stab at a few proven generalities. Here's a short list of insurance I recommend. Consider your local geography, the extent of your business dealings, your financial situation, health and safety issues, and other factors when purchasing insurance. You may want to add a few items to the list. Invest a good bit of time with a reputable insurance agent, backed by an A-rated company, who knows your community, its business environment, and real estate. I suspect that you'll need coverage in some areas you've never even considered.

 SECRET OF A MILLIONAIRE REAL ESTATE DEVELOPER

39. Protect yourself and your business with appropriate insurance coverage from day one.

Liability Coverage

Liability insurance is one of those needs that actually does apply across the board. You need it. What happens if someone walks onto your property and is seriously injured? You get sued, that's what. If the man or woman doesn't sue you, their survivors will. And if they don't, some politically aggressive, socially oriented group of activists will. These days it seems as if everybody is looking for an excuse to sue everybody else. Remember the woman who sued the fast-food chain after she bought a cup of hot coffee because she was burned when she tried to drink that hot coffee? Additionally, it seems to me that the awards for damages in these cases are escalating every year. So is the need for better insurance protection.

Even if you run your business, developments, and construction sites with the best of intentions, accidents will happen. Developers get sued. Because millionaire real estate developers know that, they prepare for the eventuality. One of their best defenses is liability insurance.

Fire Insurance

You'll most certainly need fire insurance coverage, too. It's an essential component of your overall plan. Think for a moment of how many ways a fire can start on a job site or in a building. Electrical wiring can be faulty. Electrical cords can fray, and cutting and grinding can shower an area with sparks. On cold winter days workers often build fires from scrap wood to keep warm. Hot sparks and burning embers can float all over the site. On dry summer days the heat from a tailpipe can spark a grass fire. Even if you have a no smoking policy, someone will sneak a puff or two, probably near sawdust, combustible fluids, or flammable insulation. Open flames from any number of sources can spread with alarming speed. And the list could go on for pages. Fire is a serious danger to life, limb, and the health and safety of your business. See that you're fully protected.

Flood Insurance

Flood insurance isn't as necessary as fire insurance, but more people need it than they realize. Properties that appear to be high and dry are often in officially designated floodplains. Even in these days of controlled water resources, those resources sometimes get out of their banks. The destructive power of moving water is astounding. Contact the appropriate department of your city or county government to find out if your development is in or near a floodplain before the rains come and you discover an unpleasant development courtesy of Mother Nature.

Earthquake Insurance

This type of coverage is an obvious need in such places as California for which the term "shake, rattle, and roll" was invented. Other parts of the country may not suffer as much, but they also get shaken up pretty well, too. It's not very well known, but one of the greatest earthquakes in history occurred in the eastern United States. The New Madrid quake of 1811 was 8.0 or greater on the Richter Scale. The event was so powerful that the Mississippi River reversed its course. This quake affected every part of today's continental United States, save for the far Pacific Coast. Major earthquakes in Missouri!

Oh, yeah. And lots of other places, too.

Because other parts of the country aren't hit as often as California, their buildings aren't always up to handling the effects of a big quake. The damage could be significantly worse. If you think you don't need earthquake insurance, consult your insurance professional and a couple of good local history books and think again.

Umbrella Insurance

Sometimes called "blanket coverage," umbrella insurance is designed to pick up the slack when your current liability insurance protection ends. For example, let's say you have an injury that results from a porch collapse, injuring many people on a porch or deck. This may be a multimillion dollar loss, but your liability insurance will cover only $2 million. Instead of reaching into your pockets for the additional funds, you have an additional $10 million as your umbrella coverage. This takes care of the additional expense. As a rule of thumb, I recommend that your umbrella insurance cover double the value of your personal assets.

Extended Coverage Insurance

To my mind a "what if" type of insurance is a prudent purchase. Unlike umbrella coverage, extended coverage doesn't pick up the slack from another policy. It's insurance used to cover an amazingly broad range of possible physical accidents to the property itself, incidents such as water damage from a burst water heater. Like acorns to oaks, little incidents can grow into big problems. It's best to have a backup plan in place. Ask your insurance expert for the types of extended coverage recommended for your type of development.

Worker's Compensation Insurance

This insurance is essential for developers who have employees, and what developer doesn't have employees, even if they're only temporary workers? If someone in your employ is injured on the job, your worker's compensation will come in mighty handy. Note that an employee doesn't have to be injured at the office or on the job site, just injured on the job while working for you. In many states, worker's compensation is mandatory.

Builder's Risk Insurance

Builder's risk insurance protects your job site, equipment, and materials while the project is under construction. It's a good idea to acquire this type of coverage regardless of the size of the project. Even some basic remodeling jobs would be well-served by having this type of coverage. Areas of potential harm that may be protected include fire, lightning, vandalism, smoke damage, water damage, wind and other weather damage, theft of tools or equipment or materials, materials in transit or storage, mechanical and/or electrical breakdown, sewers and drains, changes in laws or ordinances, model home and unsold dwelling coverage, and even your profit.

Title Insurance

Title insurance provides evidence that the buyer of a piece of property actually owns that property—has title to it. A developer who buys property without clear title is bucking for a suite in the funny farm. Claims on a piece of property could predate the Revolutionary War, and people can come out of the woodwork at the worst possible moment to lay claim to what you believe is your property. If you don't have clear title, the future of your development could get terribly murky.

Mortgage Insurance

This form of insurance can pay off a mortgage in the event the policy holder cannot fulfill his or her obligation. For example, if you were permanently injured in an accident and could no longer complete your projects or financial obligations, mortgage insurance would take over.

Contents Insurance

Contents insurance protects any of your property stored or used on property you're using to generate income. For example, it would protect the tractor/mower used to keep the grounds in good shape. You could also cover appliances, washers and dryers, specialized equipment, and so on.

Loss of Rents Insurance

This coverage is very handy if your development involves rental income. Some developers will go to great lengths to protect their *property* through flood, fire, earthquake, and other types of disasters. Yet, they'll neglect to protect their *profits* from the effects of such disasters. What happens to all the rental payments while your destroyed or damaged property is being repaired or replaced? Your expenses certainly continue and will probably go up significantly. Smart developers are ready for such emergencies with loss of rents insurance.

Boiler and Machinery Insurance

Consider coverage that offers protection against claims from people injured by large machinery or equipment, such as a boiler or a building's air-conditioning unit.

Vandalism Insurance

You'd better recognize and deal with the state of the culture in which we live. Empty job sites are particularly attractive to thugs who just love to steal, bend, break, tear down, rip up, and spray paint. Even buildings and property in attractive, upscale parts of town are not immune.

The Right Way to Handle an Insurance Problem

The need for insurance in real estate development will be a constant factor in the growth, development, and ongoing success of your business. Claims against you aren't a certainty, but the more you develop, the more likely you are to face one. Job sites are a natural source of accident and injury. Accidents happen inside office buildings every day. Sidewalks and doorways can become slippery slopes in wind, rain, and snow. What should you do when a problem arises?

First, don't freak out. You're a leader, and you have to act like one. Even if you're quaking on the inside, let your outside show a calmness and control that inspires confidence in everyone else. Panic and fear have a way of spreading, and when they spread from the top, the damage to morale and the organization can be devastating. No matter how bad a situation is, it's unlikely that it will match the horrible vision conjured up by your worst fears. Get a grip on yourself so that you can get a grip on the situation.

Second, get information. What happened? Who did it happen to? Where did it occur? What is the current status of the situation? If someone is hurt, apply first aid and/or call 911 for expert help. Find out exactly what's happening. Who should you contact first, 911, your lawyer, or the media? You can't make that important decision without solid information.

Third, get in touch with your insurance agent. File an accident report or whatever report or reports the situation requires. If he or she requests any additional information or documentation, start working on it immediately. If reports or interviews are necessary from other people, get them quickly and properly. Memory has a way of altering the "facts" of any given situation, so you want to respond to the event without hesitation. Your goal is to do the right thing, do it fast, and take care of business so you can get back to business.

Fourth, follow up after the situation is resolved. How you accomplish that will depend on the situation, but at least check in with the affected parties to see how he, she, they, or the situation is faring.

SECRET OF A MILLIONAIRE REAL ESTATE DEVELOPER

40. Don't let unfortunate situations develop so that they get out of hand.

Playing "What If" with Insurance

An excellent way to evaluate your potential real estate insurance needs is to play the "what if" game mentioned above in "Extended Coverage." Look around your office or office building. Take a tour of your job sites. Try to imagine all the many things that could possibly go wrong. Some of them will go wrong. What if the roof leaks over the central computer? What if a client slips on the stairs? What if there's an accident during construction? What do you do then? Once you have an idea of the potential problems and the potential ramifications of those problems, you should have at least an idea of which corrective or protective measures to take.

Playing the "what if" game today can go a long way toward preventing accidents, injuries, and insurance problems in the future. Go over your findings and any planned changes with your insurance agent. It's just possible that this little game could turn into some serious savings in the amount you pay for insurance coverage. The bottom line is still simple and basic. A safe and healthy environment for your employees, clients, and guests is also a safer and healthier environment for your business.

Finding the Best Insurance

Finding the best insurance for your specific needs begins with a twofold process. First, you have to find the best insurance carrier. Ask yourself the following questions:

- What exactly requires insurance protection?
- Why should I buy insurance for _____? (Answer this question for each item used to fill in that blank.)
- How much coverage is enough coverage? Am I sure?
- What's the price tag on that coverage?
- How much can that price escalate during my real estate development career?
- What, precisely, are the terms and conditions of coverage?
- What has been the experience of my friends and associates in real estate with that insurance company?
- How well has this insurance company responded to problems in the past?

It's easy to find a lot of insurance companies. They all advertise, and the ones that say they're real-estate savvy advertise in industry publications. Check them out by visiting their Web sites. Ask around to learn from other developers' experiences and to get references from people in the business. Get all the information you can and then move on to the next step.

Second, you have to find the best agent representing that company. This chore is identical to what you went through to find the best attorney, accountant, and financial advisor. Ask around. Get recommendations. Visit with the agent. Don't be afraid to ask tough and probing questions. It's important to get someone who can "take care of business"; specifically, it's important to find someone who will take care of your business. Get references and check them out. Then, and only then, make your decision.

Keep looking until you find the right agent working for the right company. Sometimes it won't work out that way. A great agent may be working for a so-so company or one that really doesn't excel in real estate. A great company may have only so-so local representatives. In some cases you may be in the delightful position of having a number of excellent selections. It's important to make a decision based on what's best for your company. One essential task is to get insurance quotes from different companies.

It's a good idea to shop around. It's an even better idea to continue shopping around throughout your career. Agents move from company to company. Companies change management, policies, procedures, coverage, rates, and even the quality of their service. I try to stay ahead of that game by staying in touch with the insurance industry.

Be wary of buying too much insurance. Yes, it's possible. Salespeople, regardless of what they're selling, will always try to sell more of whatever it is that they're selling. Listen to their pitch. If you've done your research and selected a good agent, his or her opinion is valuable. Still, the agent is a salesperson whose job description includes the command, "Sell." Evaluate every recommendation carefully and ask pointed questions as to why each element is necessary. It's essential to fully protect your business, but buying insurance you really don't need is just a waste of resources that could be put to better use elsewhere. When an agent offers add-ons or additional coverage, just ask the question, "Why is that a good idea?"

Make sure that you buy your insurance from a company that has earned an A rating. This means that the company is sound and is in a financial position to pay off on any claims you may make. You might get lower rates with lesser rated companies, but those companies might not be there when you need them. And if the company is there, it may not have the financial resources to back you up. In other words, buying from a company without an A rating is a crap shoot. I don't know about you, but I don't gamble with the future of my company.

And that's what insurance is all about. Ambrose Bierce in *The Devil's Dictionary* compared insurance to a game of chance. Well, business is a gamble, always. If you want to play this game, it's essential that you play by the rules. By protecting yourself with great insurance backed by a great company and with a great local agent, you will go a long way towards taking risk out of the game.

Advertising and Public Relations

The business that considers itself immune to the necessity for advertising sooner or later finds itself immune to business.

Derby Brown

Everybody Plays the PR "Game"

Millionaire real estate developers are by definition news makers. Even if they prefer to shun publicity, they have to understand advertising, public relations, and media relations because it's all part of the development job. Advertising is essential to business success. Whether you're developing an image, a community, an apartment building, a retail shopping center, or an industrial park, you'll need to attract buyers and renters. You'll need to advertise for employees, and you may at some point even find a need for advocacy advertising to get your point of view to a desired audience. Developments going up are news. Accidents on the job site are news. Promotions in your company, a relocation of corporate offices, appointments of officers to public bodies, or any number of business-related events are news. As a prominent developer you'll find that reporters, analysts, and columnists will be contacting you or your office all the time. They'll want to do stories on you, your development, your company, your problems, your successes, and God only knows what else. It's best that you understand the media, how it works, and

181

how you can best work with their representatives to give yourself as fair a shake as possible.

This is important. Regardless of your likes or dislikes, you and your business are in the public relations "game." It's important that you understand the rules so you can play to win.

The Importance of a Positive Public Image

There was a time when successful businesspeople were considered heroes of the American culture. Unless they were like mean old Mr. Potter from *It's a Wonderful Life,* the fact that they had overcome the odds, built a business or an empire, employed people, and contributed to the tax rolls and to the community, was considered sufficient reason for communitywide respect. Things have changed. Large segments of the population view business and businesspeople as the enemy or at least as a group not to be trusted. Other large segments remain more aloof and skeptical than ever before.

Developers need public support. Try getting a zoning change through the city council with a large group of angry voters outside chanting "No-no-no!" See what kind of reception you get down at city hall or in the state legislature if the news media are running editorials against your proposed development. How many top managers do you think you can attract if the front door to your office is blocked by sign-toting protesters? I don't care if you're a left-winger, right-winger, tree-hugger, industrialist, or a member of a UFO cult. Whatever position you have will be opposed by some group, and today groups in this country are quite media savvy. Part of your job is, as much as possible, to sway as much as you can of the public, and therefore the news media and politicians, to your side of the argument. Advertising, public relations, and media relations are powerful weapons in your arsenal. As with rifles or pistols, before you pull one out, you'd better know how to use it.

 SECRET OF A MILLIONAIRE REAL ESTATE DEVELOPER

41. Be media savvy.

There's always the possibility of shooting yourself in the foot. Public relations is always a loaded weapon.

Research Your Market

It's impossible to chart a course to where you're going if you haven't a clue as to where you are. Market research is an essential tool of the millionaire real estate developer. You'll conduct research for all kinds of purposes, but because this chapter is about public relations, I'll limit my comments to that rather narrow area. One of the first tasks you should perform is a SWOT analysis of your market. SWOT is an acronym for

- **S**trengths,
- **W**eaknesses,
- **O**pportunities, and
- **T**hreats.

Strengths and weaknesses are matters internal to your organization. For example, you might be well capitalized, a strength, but you might lack a strong management team, a weakness. You could have inherited a negative public image from the previous owners of a property you've just purchased, or you could have an outstanding positive image as a community leader. Each strength and each weakness will be unique to you, your organization, *and the current situation.* "Current" is a key word because your position on the public relations game board is always shifting. An image is a fickle and fragile thing. For example, you might be seen as a real force for good in the community, but the negative image of that newly purchased property could still have negative repercussions. You'll have to address the issue through some targeted advertising, public relations, and efforts to get your side of the story to the public through the media or make efforts to do all three.

Opportunities and threats are external. That new property certainly represents an opportunity. You can turn it around and turn a tidy profit while taking advantage of that opportunity. But the negative image associated with the previous owner could tarnish your reputation. That's a significant threat. Sometimes threats can also be turned into opportunities. You could pull your public relations team together to let the public know that as the new owner you're already addressing whatever problems were associated with the previous owner. More than that, you're turning that project around, creating more jobs, adding to the tax rolls, and enhancing the quality of life for everyone in the neighborhood, which makes your new purchase the best thing since sliced bread. Get the idea?

You can't get from here to there until you know precisely where here is located. Market research provides that information and in doing so helps you draw your roadmap.

Evaluate Your Media Options

Any community of any size will have some news media, and they'll be supported primarily by paid advertising. Even small towns with only a few thousand people will have a weekly newspaper, a local radio station, outdoor advertising, penny-shopper papers, and perhaps even local access advertising through a cable television company. Let's take a real brief tour of your basic media options.

Television

TV has the value of combining sight with sound, a benefit for commercial advertisers as well as the programming department. It's the nation's most popular form of entertainment and a key source of news and information. The medium reaches its audiences by broadcast, cable, and satellite. The proliferation of 24-hour news channels has created a huge news void that the cable channels (many also transmitted by satellite) have to scramble to fill. This vast amount of empty time can be viewed as a threat (lots of opportunity for news coverage of negative events) and as an opportunity (lots of air time at affordable rates to tell your side of the story). Local advertising is available on local stations, and in many markets local cut-in commercials are inserted in national programming.

The best type of television advertising, if this media is within your budget, is cable television advertising. Cable can direct your product to your local audience often for less money than the cost of radio advertising. You can choose the type of channel—family, youth, business, sports—whatever you feel is best directed at your audience. You really don't have to spend excessive amounts of money to bring your product to the public.

Radio

Prior to television, the nation tuned in to radio for the bulk of its entertainment. Lacking the visual aspects, radio is considered by many advertising persons as a challenge, but in creative hands the medium can be exploited brilliantly. In contrast to broadcast television, radio is most often "narrowcast" to specific audiences. Even programs that are nationally syndicated cater to narrow audience segments: talk radio, country western, hip-hop, rock, gospel, beautiful music, oldies channels, and in larger markets you can find even greater specialization, such as Spanish language, reggae, bluegrass, public radio, and so on.

Most stations carry news on the hour and half hour, and many of the stations will broadcast local news, sports, and weather in those breaks. That's not much time, but sometimes developers are in the news or even make the news.

If you want to spend your money on radio efficiently, choose times to air your spots just on the fringe of prime time, conveniently enough called "fringe" time in the broadcast industry. As an example, when I advertise, I like to be on "drive time" on the news station. But if I go on the air between 4:00 PM–7:00 PM, I am paying a premium for those minutes. *But,* if I chose 7:01 PM–9:00 PM, the rates drop significantly. That means I am saving almost 25 percent off the drive time rates. Think about it. I know that many people are driving between 7:01 PM–9:00 PM, and a lot of them are tuned into their favorite radio station. So I use my advertising dollars wisely, stretching them as far as they will go.

Print

Most communities have at least one major daily newspaper, and small towns often have a weekly newspaper. There's more room in a paper for advertising, news, and other information than in any other media. One of the big national newspapers ran a great ad many years ago, a reprint of a front page with a small amount of news copy highlighted in bright yellow. The copy noted that a half-hour TV news broadcast had time to carry only the amount of news highlighted in yellow. The contrast between the amount of news available on TV versus the amount carried in the newspaper was dramatic and powerful. Print media has a longer "shelf life" than broadcast media, too. The newspaper can hang around all day, and magazines may be flipped through all month long.

Many midsize and larger towns have their own city magazines, entertainment magazines, visitor's guides, sports guides, and other publications of local interest. Most of these, if not all, in any given market will be supported by advertising. Their editorial content may not be appropriate for your news releases, so be prudent with your time and resources. The announcement of your new downtown highrise office building just may not fit the editorial profile of *Swamps 'N' Gators* monthly.

Penny-shopper papers are everywhere. Their reason for being is advertising, but they'll often accept news and information. Surprisingly, these can be effective advertising vehicles for people in real estate, especially those folks in residential sales and apartment rentals. If the publication's geographical market is right, developers can often put these vehicles to good use, too.

The best way to get the most for your money is to see where most people advertise their property. In Chicago, it's the *Chicago Tribune* Sunday real estate section. Even the *Tribune* during the week has real estate advertising. But you will never see me in the weekday papers. I only want to be where the majority of my peers are. Why? Because they know, as I do, what people read. The *Chicago Sun Times,* Chicago's second-biggest daily newspaper, has never worked at all for me. Yes, they have a real estate section on Sunday, and I have been featured in stories there, but I won't drop nickel one in the paper. I want results, and that is the *Tribune.* Now I know that I will have the *Sun Times* ringing my phone telling me of their success stories. I'm sure that those success stories are valid and that a lot of their advertisers are happy, but I know what works for me. Also, most of the local neighborhood papers will do me no good either, so I just say, "no, thanks," when people call me for my advertising dollars. You should find what is most successful in your community and stick to those papers bringing you positive and verifiable results.

Outdoor

Outdoor advertising is everywhere: on the highways, on the back roads, in downtowns, and in the suburbs. Many sign types are available such as those huge panels sticking up above the interstate, as the smaller rectangular billboards that are everywhere, as "junior boards" that are small-size versions of billboards, and as signs of all sizes, shapes, and formats.

Signs are usually very prominent, but the amount of information you can convey on a sign is extremely limited. Think in terms of ten words or less. Also, your artwork, if you use any at all, must be bold and simple. The next time you drive around, pay attention to the billboards you pass. See how many of them are impossible to read. Signs are a great way to create or build awareness, but their limitations don't allow much room for selling. Be bold. Be brief. Be read.

Direct Mail

Direct mail is very expensive in terms of the cost to get one bit of information in the hands of one member of your target audience. There's an advantage, though. There's a lot of waste circulation associated with the large broadcast and print media. You pay your ad rates based on their large circulation (or audience), but there are just a whole lot of folks in that audience who are not and never will be your customers or clients. You're paying for something that really can't do you a lot of good. With direct mail, you can pretty well target your audience to precisely the individuals you need. That's a tremendous advantage that significantly compensates for the cost.

Whether you're sending out advertising or public relations materials, you'll need to be very creative. Everybody's mailbox is stuffed with all kinds of brochures, flyers, letters, and notices. You've got to stand out of the crowd or you'll be trampled by it.

A newcomer to the field is the e-mail newsletter. As more and more people go online and as more and more of them begin conducting business through the Internet, this option will inevitably grow in popularity and in effectiveness. When publishing an e-mail newsletter, always keep the interests of the reader in mind. Couch the information about you, your organization, and your developments in language that showcases all your benefits to the reader. Think of yourself as the reader and ask, "What's in it for me?" The vehicle is today the "new kid on the block," but it's one worth employing as it grows up.

Become an Author

A lot of real estate professionals buy advertising space and place ads there that appear to be editorial content offering advice from an expert. The real estate professional is the "columnist" pictured prominently in the "advertorial." There's nothing wrong or misleading about this. The newspaper or magazine will place the word "advertising" above the material. It can be an effective format for promoting your business.

But what's wrong with the real thing? I write a lot of columns, guest columns, and letters to the editor. You know a lot about your profession, your community, and the changing trends in that community. You have a lot of information that a lot of readers or listeners would love to have. Why not share it? Approach the news media editors in your area with proposals for columns, articles, features, or editorials. Make sure that your material is of legitimate interest and that your focus is on the reader's needs. Don't try to push your own business within the material unless you have a genuine example or story that directly applies to your point. Your name and company name attached to the material will be plenty.

Become a Lecturer

I am often asked to speak on real estate topics to adult education classes at local schools and universities. I recommend that you seek out as many such opportunities as you can. There are three major benefits. One, it's a good thing to do. Sharing your knowledge helps your community and does wonders for the old ego. Inquire at your local university, college, business school, and trade school to see if guest lecturers are needed. If you don't get a positive response right away, continue making the contacts over the years. Things change.

Two, you get to showcase your expertise and experience to a large group of people. It's quite possible that you'll find a number of good customers within that group. Three, beyond the possibility of finding customers, you can probably generate a number of good referrals to customers or properties.

In other words, you give and you get. That's a perfect win/win scenario.

A Few Thoughts on Advertising

I could write an entire book on advertising. I could even write an entire book just on the topic of real estate advertising. There's obviously not enough room here for much detail, but I would like to pass along a few guidelines that I hope you'll adopt in your own advertising program.

Determine Your Message Before You Advertise

I'm not very big on institutional advertising, the taking out of ads telling the world that you and/or your company is the best thing since sliced bread made contact with peanut butter and jelly. I've never believed in advertising just "to keep my name out there." For me, advertising must have a specific purpose, and that is the sale, rental, or development of real estate. That way I keep my name out there by selling my goods and services to willing buyers.

What is your message? I seriously doubt that it's, "Love me. Love my company," although we certainly see enough of that tripe out there. I bet your message is more like "Buy my property," or "Rent my space," or "Pass the bond issue." Chances are you'll always have some specific message you want to get to some audience. Formulate it carefully and precisely. Boil it down to a few words or phrases before you try to come up with a clever way of stating it in an ad. What do I really want to say?

Determine Your Audience Before You Advertise

The next obvious question is: To whom do I want to say it? For advertising to be effective it must reach the right people every time. That's key because your market can change with every project and even within the lifetime of a given project. For example, initially, your market might be defined as the city council so that you can get a zoning change that will allow your development in a specific neighborhood. That's a very narrow market that might be best addressed through the vehicles of personal contact and perhaps some direct mail efforts. You might write each councilman a personal letter. A brochure outlining the benefits of your development to the community might be included or used as a follow-up effort. Before the vote, you might even indulge in a few phone calls or even a bit of "glad-handing" in person.

Later on, after the zoning change is passed, you might want to drum up public support for the project. You could use mass media advertising to promote your new venture. You'd probably include a public relations effort to garner positive news coverage in the various news media. After the project is complete, you'll need buyers and/or renters, so advertising to the appropriate market would be in order. Mass media newspapers or broadcast media might be appropriate if your market is the general public. If the business community is your target, you might select more focused vehicles such as the local business magazine, the business section of the daily paper or weekly paper, and perhaps commercials in the news and weather programs of the local broadcast media.

Who is your audience? Which medium or combination of media best reaches that audience? And don't be fooled by ratings and circulation data. If the medium doesn't reach your specific audience effectively, it's no good to you no matter how many readers, listeners, or viewers it has.

Don't Automatically Follow the Pack

There's a tendency among people who advertise, and it's certainly prevalent among people in the advertising profession, to copy what the large, national advertisers are doing. "They're spending millions, so they must be right." My advice is to follow your mother's advice. Remember when you wanted to do something foolish and argued that "everybody's doing it?" Mom would always reply, "If all your friends jumped off the roof, would you jump with them?" That philosophy applies to advertising, too.

A lot of very expensive national promotion is the rotgut of advertising. It's a waste of time, energy, money, and sometimes the public's good will. Don't misunderstand me. A lot of it is also brilliant. I'm just saying, don't follow the pack just because there's a pack. Barking, yelping, and snapping at the consumer's heels will get you at lot of attention, but it won't earn you a lot of customers, friends, or positive "word of mouth" in the community. Consider the image of your company and your projects and consider the dynamics of your target audiences. Then, and only then decide which course to take.

Embrace Simplicity

The KISS rule, Keep It Simple, Stupid, works in almost all areas of life, and it certainly works in advertising and public relations. Wherever your ad or public relations materials are placed, they have to compete with news, information, and other advertising materials and messages. Clutter, a lot of ads placed together, is a real problem on the airways, in print, and in your mailbox. You have only a few seconds in which to grab someone's attention. If you don't get them with your headline or the first few words of your ad, you won't get them at all.

Does your ad or public relations piece say what you want it to say? Does it make the statement powerfully, emotionally, and with simplicity? Will your audience grasp it right away? If you can't say yes to the above questions, don't say yes to the ad. Go back to the drawing board and get it right before you get it in print or on the air.

A Few Words about Public Relations

Apply everything I just wrote about advertising to your public relations efforts. People who become millionaire real estate developers invest the time to develop professional public relations programs. Their efforts may never be more sophisticated than a personal letter, still one of the most powerful tools in the media arsenal. Or they may regularly send out extensive packages with four-color brochures, video presentations, interactive CD ROMs, and three-dimensional models of the new development. Regardless of the level of sophistication or expense, each effort is carefully planned and executed.

I have always been seen as an expert on self-promotion. When interviewed on TV, or when I send out press releases to the media on my projects, properties, and successes, I tell a story. I like people to know what I do. Often the first step in getting someone in the media interested in hearing my latest story is a news release. You can get any number of books on proper phrasing and formats of press releases at your local library. I advise you to study up on the right way to write and to present press releases before making the attempt. Editors are notorious for tossing poorly produced materials directly into the "round file" beneath the desk. Just for your reference, Figure 15.1 has an example from one of my recent projects.

This press release puts my name in the public eye, but it would never be seen in print or heard over the airways if it were not written in a way to arouse curiosity and keep the editors and reporters interested. I want the media to look at my material and find my story newsworthy. Because there is a lot of competition for news space out there, I want to do everything possible to make sure I earn my share.

Technology has come to your aid also. You can now send your news release instantly by using the Internet and your e-mail system. You can even attach digital photographs to the release. Digital photography is a godsend for real estate developers (and its use isn't limited to just public relations and promotions). You can take photographs, crop them to the appropriate size, and

FIGURE 15.1 Sample Press Release

PRESS RELEASE

FOR IMMEDIATE RELEASE

MARK B. WEISS SELLS
6127-6223 S. KENWOOD, Chicago, IL

6217-6223 S. Kenwood, a two-building, three-story brick renovated income property located in Chicago's Woodlawn neighborhood was sold by Mark B. Weiss Real Estate. The property was acquired after foreclosure in 1999, had been completely renovated, and was a winner of the Chicago Association of REALTORS® (CAR) "Good Neighbor Award" in 2002.

"This was excellence in vintage renovation providing lovely affordable housing in a neighborhood just south of the Midway and the University of Chicago," stated the judging panel from CAR.

As development resurgence occurred in the Woodlawn neighborhood of Chicago's South Side, these buildings, which at one time stood as an island at the time of the sellers original purchase, are now surrounded by new renovations and new developments.

The owner's attention to detail and screening of good credit tenants helped to stabilize the area, which has gained in prominence over the past few years. Mark B. Weiss Real Estate Brokerage managed the property and oversaw the renovation.

The property consisted of a six five-room, two-bedroom apartments and eighteen three-room, one-bedroom units.

Although the original properties were center-entry six-flats, the seller had obtained permits and divided the property into twelve units per building. Hot water baseboard heat with individual controls was one amenity that was installed in the building for the tenants.

The property had class nine status, which means that real estate taxes were lowered for ten years, due to the extensive renovation to improve the property.

Many of the tenants in the property were congregants of the Apostolic Church of God located at 63rd and Kenwood.

Mark B. Weiss, CCIM, was the exclusive broker in the transaction.

Although undisclosed, the sales prices exceeded the seller's expectations and set a new high for buildings in this neighborhood.

For more information and details, contact Mark B. Weiss, CCIM, at (773) 871-1818x1.

www.markbweiss.com

even enhance them with the wide range of editing technology available with basic camera/computer systems. A word of caution: think about how your photograph will be used and in what medium. Because newspapers are printed on inexpensive paper, the photographs in them appear grainy. Make sure your photo is simple, well lighted, and composed so that it can be used in the format. If you plan to send a lot of photos, invest in a tripod to steady your camera to make sure your shots are not blurred.

Public relations costs you nothing. It has a stronger effect than anything you pay for simply because the public views the information as news rather than as paid advertising. It causes you to be an expert, and the media then will find *you* to consult with on other stories. That happens to me often. That is how I became a real estate book author as well. In year 2001, I was contacted by a literary agent who had heard of me and my work through years of my constant self-promoting. She felt I was an expert capable of fulfilling a publisher's need for real estate books. This is my fifth book in three years. Not bad, if I say so myself. By being published, other doors have opened, like teaching engagements and media interviews. Because one thing always leads to another, remember the words of the wisest and most prolific of authors, Anonymous, who said, "They who have something to sell, never whisper in the well; but they who really want the dollars, stand on the roof tops and holler."

Working with the News Media

Working with reporters, columnists, and other news media personnel requires skill and tact. Too many people in real estate have too casual an attitude about getting their information carried by the news media. I think a lot of it stems from the fact that they say what they want where they want through paid advertising in the same vehicles. Their attitude is as simple as it is wrong. Because they pay money for advertising, they think they're due favorable treatment in the editorial side of the business.

Nothing could be further from the truth. Oh, there are a few exceptions where a few dollars can buy you coverage, but is that the kind of coverage you want and need? If you know you can buy "news," then so do a lot of other people who are probably doing the same thing. So, who can you really influence or impress anyway? In most media there is a solid wall between the advertising department and the editorial side. And that's a good thing. When I read my news, I want to know that I'm getting the straight story and not some PR flack's version of events. They may be owned by the same corporate entity, but you'd be wise to treat the ad department and the news department as separate entities. For all practical purposes they are.

In working with people in the news media, I've always found that honesty is the best policy. I'm available, open, and straightforward with any reporter who calls my number. Keep in mind that honest answers include: "I don't know, but I'll get back to you" or "I can't comment on that right now" and "No comment." Here in Chicago, because the news people know that I know my business, that I'm a straight shooter, and that I'll provide information or even a comment for attribution if I can, I get a lot of calls.

Consequently, I get quoted a lot in the media, and that helps build my reputation as an important individual in the real estate industry. Hey, who looks more like a millionaire real estate developer, the guy quoted in the Sunday business section or my unmentioned competitor who refused to return a reporter's call?

Avoid Public Relations Problems Whenever You Can

In some cases you may have advance notice of a public relations problem on the horizon. Your research before making the purchase should clue you in to such problems and should put you in a position to meet the challenge head on. You might have advance notice on other potential problems. For example, you'll know if you're planning a lot of layoffs in the company, if you're moving a large corporate headquarters across the country, if a very public development is going sour, or if any number of other possibilities could generate negative coverage.

When you know a public relations problem is brewing, prepare for it. Get ready. Call up your PR firm, ad agency, PR or ad department, or group of trusted advisors in order to develop a strategy to address the situation. A bit of planning and some advance action can often eliminate the effects of a problem or at least take some of the wind out of its sails and diminish its effects on your business and your developments.

Handle Public Relations Problems

Or they will surely handle you and probably in a rough or even a brutal manner. The worst public relations problems seem to come suddenly and without notice: a worker is injured on a job site; a partner in a very prominent development has financial problems and suddenly drops out of the project; the local chapter of FAB (Free America's Bricks) files a lawsuit to halt the all-brick construction of your newest commercial center. Right or wrong, frivolous or serious, lawsuits are generally the worst bad news. For one thing, regardless of your guilt or innocence they *create* bad news and PR problems. We can't foresee the future, but we still have to be prepared for what the future brings.

 SECRET OF A MILLIONAIRE REAL ESTATE DEVELOPER

42. Play the "what if" game for public relations.

Use the "what if" technique to help prepare for an unexpected, unplanned future. I play it a lot. Play it a good bit of time on your own and with your staff, too.

- What if there's an accident on a job site?
- What if one of our partners pulls out unannounced?
- What if interest rates spike?
- What if we get sued by FAB?
- What if an officer of the corporation gets involved in a scandal?
- What if we're wrongly accused of using inferior materials?
- What if . . .
- What if . . .
- What if . . .

Really stretch your imagination and encourage your staff not to hold back. Once you have a list of "what ifs," then develop strategies for handling them. This is a good policy to institute on an ongoing basis and could be a regular part of staff meetings or part of a series of meetings devoted to this one topic. You might even develop "play books" outlining the appropriate steps if certain PR problems arise. The point is to be as ready as possible to respond quickly and appropriately to any situation and to avoid the very dangerous practice of shooting from the hip.

Unfortunately, many real estate professionals do not give public relations the attention it deserves. Those are the ones generally hit hardest when PR problems slither out of the tall grass and strike. The subject may not be as vital as capitalization, legal matters, accounting, or developing a professional staff, but public relations is a vital area. How vital? Well, I agree with Arthur W. Page of Double Day, the founder of public relations as we know it, who said, "Conduct public relations as if the whole company depends on it." As you become a millionaire real estate developer, you'll learn just how true that statement is. Please. Learn that lesson early.

CHAPTER 16

Secrets of the Business You Won't Hear from Anyone Else

You can purchase a lot of real estate books, and many of them are good. Some are excellent, and, pardon the plug, I count mine in that last category. I always want to offer my readers something extra, a benefit or a bonus not found in other materials. The subject of this book lends itself quite well to that purpose. There are a number of deep secrets that I have discovered. I'd like to share them with you.

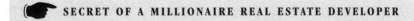 **SECRET OF A MILLIONAIRE REAL ESTATE DEVELOPER**

43. You can buy real estate with no money down if you have other collateral.

You've certainly heard about plans, schemes, and gimmicks to buy real estate with no money down. They're advertised all over the place. Well, it can be done, but only if you have "all your ducks in a row." You don't need gimmicks, schemes, or get-rich tricks. All you need is enough collateral to make your lender secure that if you default they will have something to go after to recover their money.

I used this process when I made my first condominium conversion and have found it useful in many other developments. I had excess money in a mutual fund. Cashing it in would have required me to pay significant capital gains taxes, and I believe in legally avoiding as many taxes as possible. A lender agreed to accept the mutual fund as sufficient equity to finance the acquisition and reconstruction of a vintage courtyard building.

I was able to buy real estate with no money down. Here's how the numbers worked out. The purchase price of the property was $350,000 requiring $70,000 down plus 20 percent of the anticipated construction costs of $100,000 or $20,000. Therefore, I needed $90,000 down to get the loan ($70,000 plus $20,000). The mutual fund I used as collateral was worth $120,000. The lender required that I put up the full value as the principal balance or amount of minimal equity because the value of mutual funds fluctuates according to the dictates of a fluid economy. For example, if the value had decreased 10 percent due to a fall in the stock market, I would have needed to put down more money to cover the decrease in value. I would have had to do so with each successive downward turn in the market. Using the entire value of the fund as collateral eliminated this problem.

This was a win/win scenario. The lender protected its money, and I got to finance my real estate transaction with no money down. You can do the same thing. Be wary and don't fall for the fantasies of the schemes and gimmicks. Use common sense and sound business practices. You can always buy real estate with no money down if you use other collateral such as a second mortgage, mutual fund, paid-up insurance policy, etc.

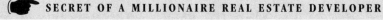

SECRET OF A MILLIONAIRE REAL ESTATE DEVELOPER

44. Trust yourself.

The only person you can really trust in the long run is yourself. This should come as no surprise, but I am continually amazed by the number of people who have to learn this lesson the hard way. You have to rely on many people in any development, and the larger the development the more people are involved. Many items on your agenda have to be verified if you're to even attempt to stay on budget and on schedule. As the developer, you are the only person who can handle those responsibilities.

If you are working another job and real estate development is, for the time being, your part-time occupation, you still have to make the investment of time to make certain that every *i* is dotted and every *t* is crossed. Being busy with other tasks is no excuse for sloppiness. In fact, the busier you are with other concerns, the greater the need for care on your part. Contractors, suppliers, and other services you need have hundreds of ways to fudge billing charges, and some of them are quite creative at it. Every dollar that goes out of the project eats away at your profits.

Read carefully and understand your loan agreements so that you are not overcharged during the term of the loan. Plan on making surprise visits to the job site to make sure the people on the job are actually working on the job. Drop in unannounced on your salespeople who have the responsibility to rent, market, or lease your property to make sure that they're adequately representing your interests. You have to verify everything that goes on. There's really no other sound choice. This isn't to say that everyone you encounter in real estate is dishonest or unworthy of your trust. That's not the case. But you can only learn who is and who isn't from lengthy experience. In the meantime watch your back. Lots of cracks can appear in any development, and it is often the goal of people and companies you work with to stuff those cracks with your money.

As the slogan says: "If there's time to do a job over, there's certainly time to do it right in the first place." It's not uncommon to arrive at a job site to discover that some phase of the project has been handled poorly and has to be redone. The expense in money, time, and frustration come right out of the developer's pocket. If you're scheduled to rent a property and if it's not ready when the tenants are set to move, you may have to pay for a temporary dwelling until they can move in. If a retail store isn't ready on time, you could not only lose a month or more of rent, you could face a lawsuit. As President Reagan said about making international agreements, "Trust, but verify."

Millionaire real estate developers learn to trust their inner voice. It's one of the best and wisest of your advisors. As you have read in this book, I learned this lesson the hard way. Regardless of what the experts say, ultimately you have to trust that inner voice and act according to what feels right.

Here's an example of what I mean. I purchased a three-flat property and hired an architect to submit drawings. The specifications for renovation included a fireplace to be located in the northeast corner of the living room. It was a small detail but important to me and my wife. When the architect submitted his drawings several weeks later, he had placed the fireplace in the southwest corner of the room. We spent a lot of time discussing the matter with him. He kept arguing that his placement was correct for the layout of the room. Because this was contrary to our desires, we asked if there were any structural reasons or any real justification for his change in placement.

With his right arm extended and his index finger pointing to the sky he said, "I am an architect! I know best."

"I am the customer. I know better. You're fired," I said. If ever there was a situation in which "the customer is always right," this was it. Because the architect, the expert, the egomaniac didn't get that, he didn't get to keep the job.

I assume that if you were insightful enough to buy this book and are insightful enough to imagine a career change, then you are a person of intelligence and courage. Remember that courage whenever you encounter some so-called authority or expert who is trying to verbally run all over you. Sometimes the experts don't understand themselves or the situation. You're a smart person, and you understand many things. You certainly know more about your real estate project than anyone else. Real estate development isn't abstract. It's practical, a matter of facts and figures. If a supplier can't explain something, he or she doesn't understand something. You'll meet a lot of people who talk a good game in this business. Just remember that you don't have to play their game.

 SECRET OF A MILLIONAIRE REAL ESTATE DEVELOPER

45. Silence can kill.

Life is communication. Communication creates knowledge. The saying that no news is good news doesn't apply to real estate development. It's important for me to hear about every aspect of every development. People don't like to be the bearer of bad news, so I call it "realistic news." Calling it that seems to take some of the sting out of the situation. Again, realistic news is something you need to hear as quickly as possible so that you can take corrective action as quickly as possible.

Holding an open house at a multiunit condo development without closing a sale is realistic news. If no one signs a contract that day, it's been a, well, realistic day. I need to know that immediately so I can get in there and tweak the situation, work with the sales agents to make better presentations, or to do whatever needs to be done to earn a signed contract and a satisfied client. I want to know what objections were raised by the attendees. Do we need to adjust the pricing? Should we alter the design in some way? What are the negative comments that repeatedly come up? If the potential buyer or renter has serious objections, I need to hear about them to take appropriate action, and I need to do it fast.

All too often when the Monday sales meeting rolls around, I ask my staff how things went during the weekend open houses. "We had a good showing" is a common response. They often don't have the heart to deliver the realistic news that no contracts were signed. That's not how I define a good showing. This is a perfect example of silence in the face of reality. It is a silence that masks the facts of a situation, and it's like burying your head in the sand.

Lender silence is an area where you need to be very cautious. I have seen some lenders drag out the loan process for weeks or months even though they know they'll never approve that application. Sometimes they're afraid of potential discrimination issues. Sometimes they have legitimate concerns about the development, the developer, or the economy. Other times they may just have a bad feeling about the project. Unfortunately, the poor developer has to invest all that money, spend all that time, and jump through all those hoops just to find out that the application is rejected. The polite silence that people are taught, the quiet that gets them through tough or embarrassing situations, isn't always a good thing. In real estate development, silence can mask a world of hurt for the developer. When it's too quiet, you might be facing the proverbial quiet before the storm. If you hear that silence, ring some bells and wake people up and get to the reality of what's going on.

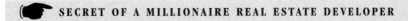 **SECRET OF A MILLIONAIRE REAL ESTATE DEVELOPER**

46. Read your documents.

We live in a busy world and receive more communications on a daily basis than many kings and queens of yesteryear received in a month of audiences. We receive letters, magazines, faxes, phone calls, e-mail, junk mail, and everything else you can imagine. There's a great temptation to skim over a lot of it. Sometimes we skim over valuable information, such as the terms and conditions found in a contract.

Please be sure that in your pursuit to become successful in real estate development that you carefully read anything that you sign. This may seem like an arduous task, but it's one you have to take on. This is especially true with contracts and agreements. When you sign those papers you are obligating yourself to the terms and conditions stated within the document. Make sure you know the full consequences of what you are signing.

The secret to success is to set your standards and abide by them. Pass on deals that are not right. Take your time. Be sure the terms of the deal make sense to you. Don't overthink everything to the point of destruction and lose opportunities. If you think it's a right decision, it probably is.

You will love your work if you feel good every day. I'm a millionaire real estate developer. I love my family, my community, my company, my work, and I feel great every day. I hope you soon share that same feeling. Now, isn't it time you really considered joining the exclusive and rewarding field of real estate development? After all, you already know the secrets.

Welcome to the club.

APPENDIXES

I believe you will find the following two documents most helpful in building your real estate development career.

It's easy to give a cursory look at the financial numbers of a real estate project and to miss the real picture. Such superficial oversight can lead to painful revelations down the road. The Investment Work Sheet in Appendix A shows you how to determine the actual return on your investment.

I've mentioned the importance of having all your "ducks in a row" when making a presentation. Appendix B shows how a presentation should look. I'm certainly not suggesting that you copy it. After all, every development, every project, every deal is different. But this document should serve as a guide to what should be included in a presentation and how that material is best presented.

Investment Work Sheet

This sample work sheet shows how money invested in real estate should work for you.

A rate of return is what we all expect when we make an investment. Money in the bank earns a safe interest rate. That rate of return is equal to the interest, after taxes, paid to the depositor by the bank.

Example:

If you deposit $100,000 @ 2.5% interest per year, you will earn $2,500. If you are taxed at a 39.5% tax rate, then after you pay your taxes you will have $1,512.50. Thus, you actually earned 1.512 % interest on your investment or a 1.512 % rate of return on your money.

Consider the following example as a rate of return in real estate with an initial cash investment of $100,000.

Example:

	Net income after expenses & taxes	Rate of return
The property acquired was purchased for $500,000 with an initial down payment of 20% of the price or $100,000 (actual cash in the deal).		
Year 1	$ 5,000	5.0%
Year 2	5,500	5.5%
Year 3	6,000	6.0%
Year 4	6,000	6.0%
Year 5	6,000	6.0%

	Net income after expenses & taxes	**Rate of return**
Cash proceeds after initial investment is returned and after taxes are paid	+80,000	80.0%
Total Return after Taxes	$108,500	

Rate of return on $100,000 over 5 years with a repayment of $108,500 = 21.60% annual return ($108,500 ÷ $100,000 = 1.0850 ÷ 5 = 0.2160 or 21.60%)

Never take the price of the property and simply look at the price sold. You only look at the actual CASH out of pocket and cash returned after taxes.

The following is typical of a presentation that you would prepare for your lenders in order to have them understand your project. I suggest adding photos of any existing structure and completed projects similar to the one you are working to finance.

LENDER PRESENTATION
PRO FORMA
WEST PARKE CONDOMINIUMS 1995
2123–25 N. Clark
Chicago, Illinois

Description: The property consists of two three-story, partially renovated Grey Stone Buildings consisting of ten units. The original structures were constructed in 1895.

The unit mix is four one-bedroom, one-bath units and four two-bedroom, two-bath units. Note that two of the two-bedroom parcels are two-level units (duplex units). There are nine parking spaces.

Construction Improvements: Over a six-month period the following will take place in order to change the use of these units from rental quality to condominium quality.

The property will be completely tuck-pointed and a new tear-off roof will be installed. Windows are new and will not require replacement.

The property has individual gas forced-air heat and air conditioning. Most apartments have new gas forced-air heating units. Those units that require replacement will be replaced. The electric circuitry fulfills current building code requirements with circuit breakers in each unit and 150 AMP per unit.

There is a nine-car parking lot to the rear of the property. Parking will be included in the price of each unit, and the ninth unit will be sold separately. The parking lot will be resurfaced.

Rehab work will include remodeling the kitchens with new cabinets, laminate counters, light fixtures, and ceramic tile floors. Sinks will be stainless steel with Mowen faucets and new Whirlpool appliances including dishwasher, refrigerator, gas range, microwave, and garbage disposal. Bathroom renovations will include new vanities, pedestal sinks, new towel bars, ceramic tile floors, Koehler toilets, and matching Koehler porcelain sinks. The tub surrounds will be ceramic tile, and the floors will be ceramic tile. New shower doors will be installed. All units will have the existing hardwood floors refinished. New electric light fixtures will be installed, including florescent fixtures in the kitchens, ceiling fans with lights in each bedroom, modest fixtures in the bathrooms, and decorative fixtures in the family rooms. Fixtures will be purchased at Home Depot or equivalent sources. In addition, all of the two-bedroom units will have individual laundry machines in each of the units. Common area hallways will have new mailboxes; they will be carpeted with marble tile entries. All doors will be replaced, and all wood moldings will be replaced. The apartments will be repainted. The common area hallways will be painted and carpeted. The first-floor apartments will include below-grade living space. The northern first-floor unit will include a second bath and in-unit laundry. The existing rear entry deck system is new.

The sell-out time is typically 18 to 24 months.

WEST PARKE CONDOMINUIMS
2123–25 N. CLARK STREET, CHICAGO, ILLINOIS
PROJECT COST ANALYSIS PROJECTION

Acquisition Price	$ 800,000
Interest 9.75%	85,800
Hard Rehab Costs	192,768 draw
Brokers' Commissions	71,890
Appraisal	2,500
Advertising	6,000
Points of Loan	9,200
Attorney's Fees	15,000
Real Estate Taxes	22,000
Title Fees	2,000
Insurance	2,500
Utilities	1,200
Property Inspection Report	3,000
Condo Survey	1,500
Contingency	22,500
Total Project Costs	$1,230,968

WEST PARKE CONDOMINUIMS
2123–25 N. CLARK STREET, CHICAGO, ILLINOIS
SALES FIGURES PER UNIT

Unit #	Sales Price	Square Footage	Bedrooms	Baths
2123 N. Clark - 1 Bilevel Duplex	$ 224,900	1,801	2	1
2123 2 Front	129,900	608	1	1
2123 2 Rear	136,900	716	1	1
2123 3 Front	134,900	646	1	1
2123 2 Rear	138,900	716	1	1
2125 1 Bilevel Duplex	239,900	2,128	2	2
2125 2nd Floor	209,900	1,246	2	1
2125 3rd Floor	209,900	1,286	2	1
Parking space #9	11,000			
Total Sell Out	$1,436,200			

WEST PARKE CONDOMINUIMS
2123–25 N. CLARK STREET, CHICAGO, ILLINOIS
PROJECT COST BREAK DOWN

Whirlpool Appliances	$ 16,128
Stove	
Refrigerator	
Dishwasher	
Disposal	
Microwave	
Washers/Dryers	
Bath Tiles	2,450
Carpet	3,200
Counters	2,400
Electric	5,000
Faucets & Bathroom Hardware	2,000
Furnace and A/C	24,500
Exterior Work Including Roof & Masonry, Tuck-point, Porch Cleaning	30,000
Plumbing	15,000
Hardware Supplies—Miscellaneous	10,000
Kitchen Tiles	2,000
Kitchen Cabinets	12,000
Labor	50,000

Light Fixtures	4,000
Masonry Work	3,500
Mirrors	1,000
Refinishing Bathtubs	2,750
Shower Doors	1,000
Sinks	2,640
Toilets	1,200
Vanities	2,000
	$192,768

GLOSSARY

AAA tenants The most creditworthy tenants as determined by national credit rating service.

abandonment The release of a claim or a right in a piece of property with the intention of terminating ownership and without giving it to anyone else.

abatement A reduction in amount.

abnormal sale A sale that is not typical within the context of the market. This can occur because of undue pressure on either the buyer or the seller or for some other reason.

absentee ownership The owner(s) of the property does (do) not physically reside on the property.

absorption rate The percent of total real estate space of a particular type that can be sold or leased in a local market.

abstract of title A history of the ownership of a parcel of land that lists transfer of title, rights, and liabilities.

accelerated depreciation The methods of depreciation for income tax purposes that increase the write-off at a rate higher than under straight-line depreciation.

acceleration clause States that upon default all of the principal installments come due immediately.

access The right to enter upon and leave property.

accessibility The ease with which one can enter and leave a property.

accrue An accumulation.

accrued depreciation Any diminishment of utility or value from the reproduction cost new of an improvement on land.

211

acquisition The process by which property ownership is achieved.

acquisition cost Total cost of purchasing an asset that includes closing costs and other transaction expenses added to the selling price.

acre A measure of land equal to 43,560 square feet.

actual authority A power that a principal has expressly conferred upon an agent or any power that is incidental or necessary to carry out the express power.

actual eviction The violation of any material breach of covenants by the landlord or any other act that wrongfully deprives the tenant of the possession of the premises.

adjusted cost basis The value of property for accounting purposes equal to the original costs plus costs of any improvements less depreciation.

adjustments In the market data approach to value, these are the additions and subtractions that are made to account for differences between market comparable properties and the subject properties being appraised.

ad valorem A prefix meaning "based on value." Most local governments levy an ad valorem tax on property.

advance Used in construction financing to provide the builder with working capital.

adverse possession A method of acquiring original title to property by open, notorious, and hostile possession for a statutory period of time; also referred to as prescription.

affidavit of title A sworn statement by seller that no defects other than those stated in a contract or deed exist in the title being conveyed.

after-tax cash flow Cash throw-off plus tax savings or minus tax liability of a project.

agency A relationship in which one party, the principal, authorizes another party, the agent, to act as the principal's representative in dealing with third parties.

agent One who acts for and in place of a principal for the purpose of affecting the principal's legal relations with third persons.

agreement An expression of mutual assent by two or more parties.

agreement of sale A contract between a purchaser and seller in which they agree on the terms and conditions of a sale. Also called a *sales contract.*

agricultural property An unimproved property available for farming activities.

air rights The right to use, control, and occupy the space above a particular parcel of land.

alienation The transfer of title from one person to another.

alienation clause A provision in a mortgage requiring full payment of the debt upon the transfer of title to the property.

ALTA Title Policy A standard title insurance policy with expanded coverage.

amortization The repayment of a financial obligation over a period of time in a series of periodic installments. In a level payment mortgage, this is the portion of the debt service that reduces the principal.

amortized loan A financial debt that is paid off over a period of time by a series of periodic payment. A loan can be fully amortized or partially amortized requiring a balloon payment to satisfy the debt at the end of the term.

anchor tenant A well-known commercial business, such as a chain store or department store, used as the primary tenant in a shopping center.

annual Yearly.

annual percentage rate (APR) The yearly cost of credit.

appeals board Many jurisdictions provide a means by which a property owner can protest a tax bill. The procedure may involve a meeting with the tax assessor or appearing before a local appeals board or board of equalization.

apportionment A division of expenses and charges between buyer and seller at the date of closing. Normally the seller pays expenses up to and including the day of closing.

appraisal An opinion or estimate of value.

appraisal process A systematic procedure of collecting and analyzing data to reach an opinion of value.

appraisal report Submitted by the appraiser to support the opinion of value.

appreciation An increase in value.

appurtenance Any right or privilege that belongs to and passes with land.

arrears Not on time; late in making payments or completing work.

as is A phrase that disclaims any promises or warranties. A person purchasing real estate "as is" takes it in exactly the condition in which it is found.

assessed value The value placed on property by the tax assessor for the purpose of determining the property tax.

assessment Placing a value on property for the purpose of levying a property tax.

assessor A tax official who determined the assessed value of property.

assignee The person receiving a contractual benefit or right.

assignment (1) the means by which a person transfers contract rights; (2) occurs when the lessee parts with the entire estate, retaining no interest.

assignor The person transferring a contractual right or benefit.

assumption fee A charge levied by a lender to a purchaser who takes title to property by assuming an existing mortgage.

assumption of mortgage A transfer of mortgage obligation to the purchaser who becomes personally liable on any deficiencies occurring in a foreclosure sale with the original borrower being secondarily liable.

attorney's opinion of title An abstract of title that an attorney has examined and has certified to be in his or her opinion an accurate statement of the facts concerning property ownership.

auction The selling of property to the highest bidder.

authorization to sell Another name for the listing agreement entered into by the seller and broker determining the rights and responsibilities of both.

balloon payment The remaining balance at maturity on a loan that has not been completely repaid through periodic payments. Once paid, the outstanding balance is zero.

base rent In percentage leases, this is the minimum due to the landlord.

basis The value of property for income tax purposes, calculated as original cost plus all capital improvements, minus accrued depreciation.

basis point There are 100 basis points in one percentage point.

beneficial interest An equitable title in property.

beneficiary (1) the lender under a deed of trust; (2) the investor in a REIT.

bilateral contract A contract in which a contract is given for the promise of another. It becomes binding when mutual promises are communicated.

bill of sale A document used to transform ownership of personal property.

blanket mortgage A mortgage that covers more then one piece of real estate.

boot In federal taxation, cash or something else of value given in the exchange of two properties when the value of one is less than the value of the other.

broker A person acting as an intermediary for another and who, for a fee, offers to perform certain functions such as those done by real estate brokers or mortgage brokers.

building code Ordinances passed by local governments that specify minimum standards of construction for new buildings. They also apply to major additions to old construction.

building permit A permit that is required by local governments before a building can be constructed or remodeled.

capital (1) in economics, a factor of production that includes all physical resources except for land; (2) in finance, a sum of money.

capital gains The tax profit realized from the sale of property.

capital gains tax A tax on profits of a qualified capital asset.

capitalization Used in the income approach to value. To capitalize income means to convert future income to present (current) value.

capitalization rate The rate of interest considered to be a reasonable return on investment, given the risk.

cash flow The sum of money generated from income producing property after all operating expenses and mortgage payments have been made.

certificate of title A document given by the title examiner stating the quality of title the seller possesses.

closed mortgage A mortgage that cannot be prepaid before maturity.

closing This is the time when title normally passes and at which prorations are made between buyer and seller in a real estate transaction. Also called *settlement.*

closing costs The expenses incurred and paid at the time of settlement on the transferring of property.

closing date Date for transferring title.

closing statement A statement prepared indicating debits and credits due on closing.

cloud on title Any claim affecting title to property.

collateral Pledged property as security for a loan.

commercial banks The largest financial intermediary directly involved in the financing of real estate. Their primary real estate activity involves short-term loans.

commercial property Income property zoned for such uses as office buildings or service facilities.

commission (1) amount due as fee for broker's performance, usually a percentage of sales price; (2) in government, a board empowered to do something.

commitment letter A promise received from a lender to supply financing if certain conditions are met.

comparable Comparable property recently sold that is used in the market data approach.

comparable sales approach *See* market data approach.

comparative analysis A method of appraising property in which the selling price of similar properties are used as the basis for estimating the value of the subject property.

comparative square foot method A technique used to estimate reproduction or replacement cost that measures the total square footage or cubic footage and multiplies this total by the current cost per square foot.

comparison method A technique for deriving a capitalization rate based on determining how much more an investor has to be compensated for a particular real estate investment in comparison to an "ideal" real estate investment.

compound interest Interest paid on interest in addition to being paid on the original principal.

condemnation The process of exercising eminent domain through court action.

conditional sale contract A contract for the sale of personal property in which title is retained by the seller until the conditions of the contract have been met.

condominium A legal form of ownership that involves a separation of property into individual ownership elements and common ownership elements.

confirmation of sale The court's approval of price, terms, and conditions of a sale ordered by the court.

consideration Anything of value offered to induce someone to enter into a contractual agreement.

construction loan A mortgage loan that provides the funds necessary for the building or construction of a real estate project.

constructive eviction Occurs when the tenant's use of the premises is substantially disturbed or interfered with by the landlord's actions or failure to act where there is a duty to act.

constructive notice The knowledge that the law presumes a person has about a particular fact irrespective of whether the person knows about the fact or not.

consumer price index (CPI) An index prepared by the Bureau of Labor Statistics to measure changes in price levels of a predetermined mix of consumer goods and services. This index is often used by owners of commercial real estate to determine increases in rent.

conventional mortgage A loan made without any government agency guaranteeing or insuring the mortgage.

conveyance The transfer of title to land from one party to another.

cooperative A form of property ownership in which a corporation is established to hold title in property and to lease the property to shareholders in the corporation.

cost approach A method of estimating value based on the economic principle of substitution; the value of a building cannot be greater than the cost of purchasing a similar site and constructing a building of equal utility.

cost basis The value of property for accounting purposes; equal to the original price plus all acquisition expenses.

co-tenants A co-owner of a property interest or estate.

date of appraisal The date as of which the opinion of value is based.

debit Money owed.

debit coverage ratio Ratio that is calculated by dividing the annual net operating income by the annual debt service of a mortgage loan.

debt financing The use of borrowed funds to make a real estate purchase.

debt service An installment payment that includes both interest and amortization of principal.

declining-balance depreciation An accelerated depreciation method in which, after the depreciation is taken, the remaining depreciable balance is the base for calculating the subsequent year's depreciation.

decree of foreclosure A court order making a foreclosure effective.

deduction A legal adjustment to reduce taxable income.

deed A written instrument, usually under seal, that contains an agreement to transfer some property interest from a grantor to a grantee.

deed in lieu of foreclosure Used by the mortgagor who is in default to convey the property to the mortgage in order to eliminate the need for a foreclosure.

deed in trust Used to convey property to a trustee in a land trust.

deed of release Given by lien holders, remaindermen, or mortgagees to relinquish their claims on the property.

deed of surrender Used to merge a life estate with a reversion or remainder.

deed of trust A deed to real property that serves the same purpose as a mortgage, involving three parties instead of two. The third party holds title for the benefit of the lender.

default The failure to perform a contractual obligation or duty.

defect in title Any lien, claim, or encumbrance on a particular piece of real estate that has been properly recorded in the public records. Recorded defects impair clear title and may result in the title being unmarketable.

deferred interest mortgage Under this mortgage, a lower interest rate and thus a lower monthly mortgage payment is charged. Upon selling the house, the lender receives the deferred interest plus a fee for postponing the interest that would normally have been paid each month.

deferred maintenance Needed repairs that have not been made.

deficiency judgment A personal claim based on a judicial order against the debtor. This occurs when a property fails to bring in a price at the foreclosure sale that covers the mortgage amount.

depreciation A decrease in value due to physical deterioration, or functional or economic obsolescence.

depreciation (tax) Deduction based on some percentage of the building value that is used to reduce the tax liability of an owner of qualified property.

deterioration A loss in value due to wear and tear, by actions of the natural elements, or use.

discounting The process of adjusting a sum to take into account the time value of money.

discount points A fee charged by the lender at settlement that results in increasing the lender's effective yield on the money borrowed. One discount point equals one percent of the loan amount.

down payment The amount paid by the purchaser that when added to the mortgage amount equals the total sales price. At time of closing, this is referred to as *equity*.

earnest money A sum of money given to bind an offer of agreement.

easement A right to limited use of enjoyment by one or more persons in the land of another.

easement appurtenant An easement created to benefit a particular tract of land.

easement by implication Occurs because of necessity, such as the conveyance of a landlocked property.

easement in gross A personal right to use the land of another.

economic base analysis A technique by which a relationship is determined between basic and nonbasic industries to forecast future economic growth in the community.

economic life The time period over which an improvement to land earns more income than the cost incurred in generating the income.

economic obsolescence A loss in value due to factors outside the subject property, such as changes in competition or surrounding land use. Also referred to as *locational obsolescence.*

economic rent The amount of rental that a building would receive if set by the market as opposed to contract rent set by the lease.

effective gross income Income received from the property before the deductions for operating expenses. Also called *gross income.*

effective interest rate The percentage rate of interest actually being paid by a borrower.

eminent domain The right of government to acquire property for a public purpose after paying just compensation.

encroachment The extension of some improvement or object across the boundary of an adjoining tract.

encumbrance Any interest in or claim on the land of another that in some manner burdens or diminishes the value of the property.

Environmental Protection Agency (EPA) The federal agency that oversees and enforces federally enacted minimum standards dealing with environmental protection.

escalation clause (1) in finance, permits the lender to raise the interest rate upon the occurrence of certain stipulated conditions; (2) in leasing, permits the lessor to raise lease payments upon the occurrence of certain stipulated conditions.

escrow agent An independent third party bound to carry out the written provisions of an escrow agreement.

estoppel The prevention of a person's denying or alleging a fact because it is contrary to a previous denial or affirmation.

exclusive-agency listing The owner employs only one broker but retains the right to personally sell the property and thereby not pay a commission. However, if anyone other than the owner makes the sale, the listing broker is still entitled to the commission stipulated.

exclusive-right-to-sell listing Under this listing arrangement, the broker employed is entitled to a commission no matter who sells the property during the listing period.

Federal Deposit Insurance Corporation (FDIC) A federal agency established to insure the deposits in member commercial banks.

fiduciary A person who essentially holds the character of trustee. A fiduciary must carry out the duties in a manner that best serves the interest of the party for whom the fiduciary relationship is established.

financing Acquisition of borrowed capital.

first lien Claim with highest priority against property. Also known as a *senior lien.*

first mortgage A mortgage on real estate in which the lender's rights are superior to the rights of subsequent lenders.

first right of refusal A provision requiring an owner to allow a specified person or group the first chance to purchase property at a fair market price before it can be offered to a third party; commonly used in condominiums and cooperatives.

flat lease One where the rent payment remains the same throughout the term of the lease.

flexible loan insurance program (FLIP) A financing technique in which cash is deposited in a pledged, interest-bearing savings account where it serves as both a cash collateral for the lender and as a source of supplemental payments for the borrower during the first few years of the loan.

floor area ratio (FAR) Indicates the relationship between a building area and land. For example, a 2:1 FAR means that two square feet of floor space may be constructed on one square foot of land.

foreclosure A legal procedure to levy on pledged property used to secure a debt under a mortgage or other lien.

front foot A property measurement for purposes of valuation that is measured by the front footage on the street line.

fully amortized mortgage A method of loan repayment in which the dollar amount of each payment is the same. The first part of each payment is interest and the remainder reduces the principal. Over the life of the mortgage, the outstanding balance is reduced to zero.

functional obsolescence A loss in value due to conditions within the structure that make the building outdated when compared with a new building.

future interest Present estate with right of possession postponed into the future; for example, a remainder following a life estate.

gap financing A loan covering the time period between when the construction loan is due and when the conditions set by the permanent lender have not been met.

general warranty deed Contains covenants in which the grantor formally guarantees that good and marketable title is being conveyed.

grandfather clause Creating an exemption from application of a new law due to previously existing circumstances.

grantee Purchaser or donee receiving title to property.

grantor Owner making conveyance of title or interest in property.

gross income The actual income received from property before the deduction for any expenses.

gross income multiplier (GIM) A method of appraising income producing property based on a multiple of the annual gross income. Also called *gross rent multiplier.*

gross leasable area Total area on which rent is paid by tenants.

gross lease A lease in which the landlord, not the tenant, is responsible for property tax, maintenance, repairs, and other operating costs.

gross rent multiplier *See* gross income multiplier.

ground lease A lease of land, usually for a long term.

ground rent A payment made by the tenant under a ground lease.

housing codes Local government codes that specify minimum standards that a dwelling unit must meet.

improved land Any land to which improvements, such as roads or buildings, have been made.

income approach A traditional means of appraising property based on the assumption that value is equal to the present worth of future rights to income.

income property Property that generates income for its owner; for example, an office building or apartment complex.

increasing and decreasing returns This economic principle states that the addition of more factors of production will add higher and higher amounts to net income up to a certain point, which is the point where the maximum value of the asset has been reached; any further addition of factors of production will do nothing to increase the value.

incumbrance *See* encumbrance.

incurable depreciation Elements of a structure that are neither physically possible nor economically feasible to correct.

independent contractor One whose time and effort are regulated by the individual and not under the direction or control of others.

installment sale A means of deferring the paying of capital gains taxes until the installment payments are actually received.

insurance coverage The total amount of insurance protection carried.

internal rate of return Equating the work of future benefits to the present worth of the investment. Also referred to as *discounted cash flow.*

land lease In certain parts of the country, the land under residential real estate is leased through a long-term lease agreement whereby the owner of the land receives periodic rent for the use of the land.

landlocked Completely shut in by adjoining parcels of land with no access to public roads.

landlord The owner or lessor of property.

land trust A device whereby property is transferred to a trustee under a trust agreement.

latent defect A defect that cannot be discovered by ordinary inspection.

lease An agreement by which a landlord gives the right to a tenant to use and to have exclusive possession but not ownership of realty for a specified period of time in consideration for the payment of rent.

leased fee The landlord's interest in leased property.

leasehold The interest that the tenant has created by a lease.

lease purchase agreement An arrangement whereby part of the rent payment is applied to the purchase price and when the prearranged total amount has been paid, title is transferred.

legal benefit Consideration that occurs when one receives a promise, act, or forbearance to act to which a person is not legally entitled.

legal description A written description of a parcel of land that locates it precisely.

lessee Tenant.

lessor Landlord.

leverage Using borrowed capital to finance the purchase of real estate or other assets.

levy (1) imposition of property tax; (2) in executing a lien, obtaining money by the sale of property.

license A personal privilege to go upon the land of another; not considered an interest in land.

licensee Anyone, either a broker or salesperson, licensed to broker real estate.

lien A legally recognized right to enforce a claim or charge on the property of another for payment of some debt, duty, or obligation.

lienee The person whose property is burdened by the lien.

like-kind property Property that qualifies for a tax-free exchange.

limited partnership An entity with a general partner and one or more passive investors, called limited partners.

line of credit The extent that an individual may borrow from a bank without further need for approval.

listing contract An employment agreement between an owner and broker defining the duties and rights of both parties.

loan closing When all conditions have been met, the loan officer disburses funds and authorizes the recording of the mortgage.

loan commitment A contractual agreement from a lender to finance a certain amount of the purchase price.

loan correspondent A person who negotiates and services loans for out-of-state lenders.

loan origination fee A charge incurred by a borrower to cover the administrative costs of the lender in making the loan.

loan processing Steps taken by a lender to complete a loan transaction.

loan-to-value ratio The relationship between the amount borrowed and the appraised value of the property.

location (1) a particular surface on the earth that is defined by legal description; (2) how a particular site relates to a surrounding land use pattern.

locational obsolescence *See* economic obsolescence.

long-term capital gain The gain realized from the sale or exchange of an asset held for more then one year.

market The economic function of bringing buyers and sellers together through the price mechanism.

market value The price at which a willing buyer and a willing seller will agree upon where neither is under any undue pressure and both are negotiating at arms length with complete knowledge of the market.

misrepresentation An innocent or negligent misstatement of a material fact detrimentally relied upon by the other party.

month-to-month tenancy A lease that has a term of one month but is renewable for successive months at the option of both parties.

mortgage The secondary financing obligation in which the borrower or mortgagor agrees to pledge property to secure the debt represented by the promissory note or bond.

mortgage banker A financial middleperson who, in addition to bringing borrower and lender together, makes loans, packages them, and sells the packages to both primary and secondary investors.

mortgage broker A person who brings together the user of capital, borrower, and the supplier of capital, lender. For this service, a finder's fee is usually paid by the borrower.

mortgage correspondent A person authorized to represent a financial institution in a particular geographic area for the purpose of making loans.

mortgagee A lender who receives a pledge of property to secure a debt.

mortgagee in possession Lender who has taken over property after default for the purpose of collecting rents and conserving the property until foreclosure.

narrative appraisal The report compiled by an appraiser stating an opinion of value based on data and the appraisal methods used in deriving the estimate of value.

net income (net operating income or NOI) Gross income less all operating expenses. NOI is used in the income approach to value.

net leasable area The part of total area leased that is exclusively used by a tenant, normally excluding such areas as hallways, washrooms, etc.

net lease Imposes on the lessee an obligation to pay such costs as property taxes, special assessments, and insurance premiums as agreed to between the parties.

net listing The broker agrees to sell the property in order to achieve a net price to the owner and anything that is received above the net price is the broker's commission. A net listing is prohibited by the licensing law in many states.

nominal interest rate The rate of interest stated in the contract.

nonrecourse loan The sole security for such a loan is the property pledged and, on the basis of agreement, the borrower cannot be held personally responsible.

obsolescence A loss in value because of a decrease in the usefulness of property due to decay, changes in technology, or people's behavior patterns and tastes.

occupancy Physical possession of real estate.

occupancy rate The ratio of the space rented to the total amount of space available for rent.

offer A promise conditioned upon some requested for act or promise.

offer and acceptance The necessary elements of mutual assent, for example, an agreement of one party to buy and another party to sell.

open-end mortgage A loan containing a clause that allows the mortgagor to borrow additional money without rewriting the mortgage.

open listing An agreement between an owner and a broker giving the broker the nonexclusive right to sell the property.

open mortgage A mortgage without a prepayment clause.

operating expenses Expenses incurred in the day-to-day operation of property that are subtracted from gross income to derive net income.

opinion of title *See* attorney's opinion of title.

option A right that is given for consideration to a party, optionee, by property owner, optionor, to purchase or lease property within a specified time at a specified price and terms. An option is irrevocable by the optionee and will not be extinguished by death or insanity of either party.

overimproved land Occurs when the owner combines more factors of production inputs with the land that can be profitably absorbed.

participation mortgage An agreement between a mortgagee and a mortgagor that provides the lender with a certain percentage of ownership in the project once the lender makes the loan.

partition The dividing of real estate held by two or more people that results in each of the parties holding individual or severalty ownership.

percentage lease The lessor receives a percentage of the gross sales or net profits as the rental payment for the lease of the property.

personal property Movables that are not annexed to or part of the land. Also referred to as *chattels.*

physical deterioration The loss in value due to wear and tear of the structure.

physical life The normal or expected time over which an asset such as a building should last.

planned unit development (PUD) A type of exception or special use permitted under many modern zoning ordinances allowing a mixture of different land uses or densities. Also referred to as *community unit plan.*

plat A map showing the division of land into lots and blocks.

plat books Located in the public records, these books identify parcels of property that have been subdivided into lots and blocks.

points *See* discount points.

population density The number of people in a given area.

prepaid expenses Payments made by the purchaser at settlement to provide for future charges such as property taxes and mortgage insurance.

prepayment clause A section in a mortgage note that permits the borrower to pay without penalty the outstanding balance before the due date.

prepayment penalty The charge levied by the lender for paying off a mortgage prior to its maturity date.

prescriptive easement An easement obtained by the open, hostile, and continuous use of the property belonging to someone else for the statutory period of time.

present value The worth in today's dollars of a future income stream and/or reversion at a given discount rate.

price An amount usually expresses in terms of money paid for property.

primary financing The loan that has the first priority.

prime rate The interest rate charged to a lender's AAA customers. This is normally the base from which other interest rates are derived.

procuring cause The actions by a broker that result in the owner being able to make a sale.

promissory note The primary legal financing obligation in which the borrower promises to pay back a sum of money borrowed.

purchase and leaseback The simultaneous buying of property and the leasing of it back to the seller.

purchase money mortgage A mortgage given by the seller to the buyer to cover all or part of the sales price.

rate of return A percentage relationship between the investment price or equity invested and the composite return.

Real Estate Settlement Procedures Act (RESPA) A law that covers most mortgage loans made on one-unit to four-unit residential property. It requires the lender to provide the loan applicant with pertinent information so that the borrower can make informed decisions as to which lender will be used to finance the purchase.

redemption period The right of a mortgagor to make good on the default within a specified time and receive the property back.

refinancing A description of an extension of the existing financing either through the same lender or through a new financial arrangement.

release clause A stipulation that, upon the payment of a certain percentage of a loan, certain lots will be removed from the blanket lien held by the lender.

renegotiable rate mortgage A renegotiated loan where the maturity is fixed (for example, 30 years) but the interest rate, and hence the monthly payment, is renegotiated periodically (for example, every three years or five years).

rent The payment made for the use of land.

rent concession A discount lowering the actual cost of a lease to a tenant.

rent control In certain geographic locations, laws have been passed that impose limitations on how much rent can be charged and what percentage increase can be levied by the landlord.

replacement cost The cost of substituting a similar structure with utility equivalent to the subject property but constructed with modern materials.

right of way An easement allowing someone to cross over a parcel of land.

run with the land Certain restrictions, easements, and covenants are part of the ownership of land and thus are not terminated when title is transferred but remain in effect from owner to owner.

sale-leaseback A technique used by owners of property as a means of raising capital. The process involves the simultaneous selling and leasing back of the property usually through a net lease.

sales contract An agreement in which the buyer and seller agree to the terms and conditions of the sale of property.

Savings Association Insurance Fund (SAIF) Insures deposits of savings associations. Operates through the Federal Deposit Insurance Corporation (FDIC). Replaced FSLIC in 1989.

second mortgage A mortgage subordinate to a first mortgage. Also referred to as a *junior mortgage.*

security deposit A sum of money given to assure the performance of an obligation.

setback lines A requirement in zoning ordinances in which all structures are to be a minimum distance from property lines.

specific performance An equitable remedy in which the court orders the contract to be performed as agreed to by the parties.

straight-line depreciation A method of computing depreciation for income tax purposes in which the difference between the original cost and the salvage value is deducted in installments evenly over the depreciable life of the asset.

strict foreclosure When a purchaser defaults under a mortgage, the seller acquires title to land and wipes out the mortgagor's equity.

subject to mortgage When a person purchases property and takes over the mortgage payments, no personal liability is undertaken by the purchaser.

sublease The transfer wherein the original lessee retains a reversion.

survey The process by which a parcel of land is measured.

take-out commitment An agreement by a permanent lender to provide the permanent financing for a real estate project when a certain event occurs, normally the completion of the project.

taxation The right of government to require contribution from citizens to pay for government services.

tax base The total tax-assessed value of all real property in a particular jurisdiction.

tax certificate A document given to the purchaser at a tax sale auction that entitles the holder to a tax deed or a treasurer's deed at the end of the tax redemption period.

tax deed A deed issued when property is sold to satisfy delinquent taxes.

tax-free exchanges A method of deferring capital gains taxes by exchanging one qualified property for another qualified property.

tax rate The rate, normally stated in units of $100, multiplied by the assessed value of property to determine the amount of the property tax due.

tax roll Located in the public records, this identifies each parcel of land, the owner of record, and the assessed value of the property.

tax sale Foreclosure of an unpaid tax lien in a public sale.

tax shelter Shielding income or gains from income tax liability.

tenancy The possession of an estate.

tenancy at sufferance A tenancy that is created when one is in wrongful possession of realty, even though the original possession may have been legal.

tenancy in common A form of concurrent ownership where two or more persons hold separate titles in the same estate.

tenancy in partnership A multiple form of ownership where the property is held in a lawful business venture.

tenant One who has the legal right to occupy the property of another under an agreement to pay rent.

tenement Property held by a tenant.

term mortgage (straight term) A method of financing in which interest only is paid during the time of the loan. At maturity, generally five years or less, the entire principle is due.

time value of money Based on the idea that because money is assumed to earn interest, a dollar today is considered to be more valuable than a dollar a year from today.

title The legally recognized evidence of a person's right to possess property.

title company A company that examines the public records to determine the marketability of an owner's title.

title insurance A policy that protects the insured against loss or damage due to defects in title.

topographic map Map showing changes in elevation through contour lines.

topography A description of surface features of land.

trade fixtures Personal property used in business that has been annexed to real property and is removable by the owner.

trading on the equity Increasing the rate of return on the owner's equity by borrowing part or the entire purchase price at a rate of interest less than the expected rate of return generated on the net income of the property.

trustor The person who creates a trust and gives the instructions to the trustee. Also called a *settlor.*

underimproved land When a parcel of land can profitably absorb more units than are currently being employed.

undisclosed principal When a third person is not advised of the existence of an agency relationship, the unknown person for whom the agent is acting is called an undisclosed principal.

undivided interest The interest of co-owners in which individual interest is indistinguishable.

uninsurable title When a title insurance company refuses to insure due to some present claim or encumbrance.

utility (1) the usefulness or satisfaction received from a good or service; (2) various services such as electricity, water, and gas.

waiver The renunciation of a claim or privilege.

warranty An assurance that defects do not exist.

warranty deed A deed in which the grantor makes formal assurance as to quality of title.

water table The distance from ground level to natural groundwater.

wear and tear The lessening in value of an asset due to ordinary and normal use.

wrap-around mortgage A junior mortgage that provides an owner additional capital without refinancing the first mortgage.

yield The interest earned by an investor on the investment.

yield to maturity The total return to the investor if the investment is held to total term.

zoning A police power device that allows for legislative division of space into districts and imposition of regulations prescribing use and intensity of use to which land within each designated district may be put.

zoning ordinance A zoning law passes by a local government that consists of a text of regulations and a map.

INDEX

ABOUT THE AUTHOR

Mark B. Weiss Real Estate Brokerage, Inc.

Since 1988, *Mark B. Weiss Real Estate Brokerage, Inc.* has maintained a well respected national reputation as a full service real estate firm.

Mark B. Weiss Real Estate Brokerage, Inc. is located in the Lincoln Park neighborhood of Chicago's north side and services the wide variety of real estate needs of property owners and buyers throughout Northern Illinois.

The real estate expertise of *Mark B. Weiss Real Estate Brokerage, Inc.* includes services for corporations, municipal institutions, and lenders. We have preformed duties as receiver, managing agent, mortgagee in possession, leasing agent, and of course as successful real estate sales brokers and agents.

Mark B. Weiss Real Estate Brokerage, Inc. has sold a spectrum of property types, including single-family homes, condominiums, townhomes, commercial property, shopping centers, apartment buildings and apartment complexes, office buildings, industrial buildings, partially complete residential and mixed-use developments, vacant land, and condominium developments.

If you are a single person looking for your first home, a family looking to move from a condominium to a house, an investor looking for an apartment building, a business looking to purchase a factory, a developer looking for a site to build new housing, or an institution looking for a manager for a shopping center in foreclosure, Mark B. Weiss Real Estate Brokerage, Inc., is your Realtor of choice.

Mr. Mark B. Weiss, *CCIM*, President

Mark B. Weiss began the company bearing his name in 1988. Over the years, *Mark B. Weiss Real Estate Brokerage, Inc.* has taken a prominent role and become well recognized nationally as a leader in the sale of commercial and investment property for financial institutions, private owners, corporations, and trusts, and as a developer of vintage property renovations throughout Chicago's neighborhoods.

A graduate of Von Steuben High School and DePaul University, Mr. Weiss is immediate past president of the Lincoln Park Builder's Club and a member of the Rogers Park Builder's Club and the Edgewater Uptown Builders Club. From 2000 to 2003, Mr. Weiss was a member of the board of directors of the Chicago Association of Realtors and served as the chairman of the association's Commercial Committee from 2000 to 2002. Mr. Weiss is a member and past director of the Illinois CCIM Chapter, a member in perpetuity and past director of the Chicago Real Estate Council, a member of the National Association of Realtors, the Realtors National Marketing Institute, the Real Estate Investment Association, the National Association of Bankruptcy Trustees, the National Association of Auctioneers, the Lincoln Park Chamber of Commerce, and the Andersonville Chamber of Commerce. Mr. Weiss has been awarded continuously since 2000 the "Good Neighbor Award" from the Chicago Association of Realtors for excellence in vintage renovation of historical residential properties located in many of Chicago's neighborhoods. Mr. Weiss began his business career when he was 19 years old in 1972 when he conceived the idea and then opened the Uncle Dan Army-Navy Stores in Chicago and began their mail order catalog business.

In 1997, Mr. Weiss helped organize and found NCB Holdings. He currently serves on the holding company board of directors of NCB Holdings. NCB holdings is the holding company of the New Century Bank, which was chartered in 1998. Mr. Weiss is a board member of Ontario Street Investments, a financial planning and investment firm, also part of NCB Holdings.

Mr. Weiss currently serves on the City of Chicago Building Department's Permit Center Advisory Board.

Mr. Weiss has taught at the Latin School of Chicago's Live and Learn program and at the Learning Annex in both Minneapolis and Los Angeles. He has moderated the Lincoln Park Builders Club Annual Forum on more than one occasion.

Mr. Weiss is the author of five real estate books: *Landlording and Property Management, The Everything Home Buying Book,* and *Flipping Properties,* published by Adams Media in Avon, Massachusetts, and *Condos, Townhomes, and Co-ops* and *Secrets of a Millionaire Real Estate Developer,* published by Dearborn Trade Publishing in Chicago. You can find his books in bookstores everywhere in North America. He is currently working on sixth title for release in Fall 2005.

Mr. Weiss is a CCIM, a Certified Commercial Investment Member, of the Commercial Investment Real Estate Institute of the National Association of Realtors. CCIMs are experts in the disciplines of commercial and investment real estate. The CCIM designation is awarded to real estate professionals who have completed 240 hours of graduate-level courses in financial analysis, commercial brokerage, market analysis, tax planning, managing and marketing troubled assets, decision analysis, and negotiation, and who have fulfilled professional experience requirements and passed a national exam. Of the estimated 200,000 commercial real estate practitioners nationwide and in Canada, approximately 6,000 currently hold the CCIM designation.

Mr. Weiss is often appointed Receiver in Cook County and DuPage County and has frequently been retained as an expert witness in legal cases involving a variety of private, bankruptcy, and disputed real estate matters.

Mr. Weiss has been actively engaged in selling property using the auction method of sale as well. Mr. Weiss is well versed in traditional sales as well as sealed bid and public call auctions. Mr. Weiss acts in the capacity of the auctioneer as well as auction event coordinator.

Because of his celebrity and expertise in the field of real estate, Mr. Weiss often appears on both radio and television programs as a real estate expert for interviews and panel discussions and is consulted as a "go-to guy" who is often quoted on Fox TV, public television, in *Time*, the *Chicago Sun-Times, Chicago Magazine, The Chicago Tribune*, CBS Market Watch.com, *Woman's World, The Estates Gazette*, UK, Realtor Publications as well as other newspapers and publications both national and international.

Partial Client List

Government Agencies

Cook County Public Guardian • Resolution Trust Corp (RTC) • Federal Deposit Insurance Corp (FDIC)

Lending Institutions

Aetna Bank • Bank of Chicago Banc Group • Bank of Ravenswood-Belmont National Bank • Bridgeview Bank • Canada Life • Citicorp • Commercial National

Bank • Cole Taylor Bank • Community Bank of Ravenswood • Continental Bank • Country Life • Devon Bank • Fireman's Fund Insurance • First Chicago • First Nationwide • First Bank of Minneapolis • Harris Bank • Heller Financial • Hyde Park Bank • Horizon Savings • Lincoln National Bank • Manufactures Bank • MB Financial • Northern Trust • Nations Credit • Pathway Financial • Richmond Bank • River Forest Bank • Security Federal Savings • Superior Bank • Uptown National Bank • Water Tower Bank • Wells Fargo Bank

Real Estate Firms

Dearborn Parkway Realty • Cagan Realty Group • ICM Realty • LR Realty

Businesses

Contract Cleaning and Maintenance • Phoenix Electric • American Auto Seat Cover • Children's Memorial Hospital—Polk Brothers • Copygraph Corp.• Grommes Precision Electric • Disco Machine • Sea World Corp • Keller Orthotics • Methodist Home and Hospital of Chicago • AAA Drive Shaft • Rexx Rugs • Coin Operated Laundry Systems

Attorneys at Law

Rosenthal and Schanfield • Wilson & McIlvaine-Schmidt and Salzman, Ltd. • Garfield and Merel, Ltd. • Holleb and Coff - Hauselman & Rappin Ltd. • Clausen Miller • Levenfeld, Pearlstein • Donald Schultz • Ruff, Weidenaar & Reidy, Ltd. • Evans, Loewenstein

Receiver

Circuit Court of Cook County • Circuit Court of DuPage County

Share the message!

Bulk discounts
Discounts start at only 10 copies and range from 30% to 55% off retail price based on quantity.

Custom publishing
Private label a cover with your organization's name and logo. Or, tailor information to your needs with a custom pamphlet that highlights specific chapters.

Ancillaries
Workshop outlines, videos, and other products are available on select titles.

Dynamic speakers
Engaging authors are available to share their expertise and insight at your event.

**Call Dearborn Trade Special Sales at
1-800-621-9621, ext. 4444,
or e-mail trade@dearborn.com**

Dearborn™
Trade Publishing
A **Kaplan Professional** Company